BEHAVIOR
THERAPY AND
RELIGION

SOME OTHER VOLUMES IN THE
SAGE FOCUS EDITIONS

8. **Controversy (Second Edition)**
Dorothy Nelkin
21. **The Black Woman**
La Frances Rodgers-Rose
31. **Black Men**
Lawrence E. Gary
32. **Major Criminal Justice Systems (Second Edition)**
George F. Cole, Stanislaw J. Frankowski, and Marc G. Gertz
41. **Black Families (Second Edition)**
Harriette Pipes McAdoo
51. **Social Control**
Jack P. Gibbs
54. **Job Stress and Burnout**
Whiton Stewart Paine
57. **Social Structure and Network Analysis**
Peter V. Marsden and Nan Lin
58. **Socialist States in the World-System**
Christopher K. Chase-Dunn
60. **The Costs of Evaluation**
Marvin C. Alkin and Lewis C. Solmon
63. **Organizational Theory and Public Policy**
Richard H. Hall and Robert E. Quinn
64. **Family Relationships in Later Life**
Timothy H. Brubaker
65. **Communication and Organizations**
Linda L. Putnam and Michael E. Pacanowsky
66. **Competence in Communication**
Robert N. Bostrom
67. **Avoiding Communication**
John A. Daly and James C. McCroskey
68. **Ethnography in Educational Evaluation**
David M. Fetterman
69. **Group Decision Making**
Walter C. Swap and Associates
70. **Children and Microcomputers**
Milton Chen and William Paisley
71. **The Language of Risk**
Dorothy Nelkin
72. **Black Children**
Harriette Pipes McAdoo and John Lewis McAdoo
73. **Industrial Democracy**
Warner Woodworth, Christopher Meek, and William Foote Whyte
74. **Grandparenthood**
Vern L. Bengtson and Joan F. Robertson
75. **Organizational Theory and Inquiry**
Yvonna S. Lincoln
76. **Men in Families**
Robert A. Lewis and Robert E. Salt
77. **Communication and Group Decision-Making**
Randy Y. Hirokawa and Marshall Scott Poole

78. **The Organization of Mental Health Services**
W. Richard Scott and Bruce L. Black
79. **Community Power**
Robert J. Waste
80. **Intimate Relationships**
Daniel Perlman and Steve Duck
81. **Children's Ethnic Socialization**
Jean S. Phinney and Mary Jane Rotheram
82. **Power Elites and Organizations**
G. William Domhoff and Thomas R. Dye
83. **Responsible Journalism**
Deni Elliott
84. **Ethnic Conflict**
Jerry Boucher, Dan Landis, and Karen Arnold Clark
85. **Aging, Health, and Family**
Timothy H. Brubaker
86. **Critical Issues in Aging Policy**
Edgar F. Borgatta and Rhonda J.V. Montgomery
87. **The Homeless in Contemporary Society**
Richard D. Bingham, Roy E. Green, and Sammis B. White
88. **Changing Men**
Michael S. Kimmel
89. **Popular Music and Communication**
James Lull
90. **Life Events and Psychological Functioning**
Lawrence H. Cohen
91. **The Social Psychology of Time**
Joseph E. McGrath
92. **Measurement of Intergenerational Relations**
David J. Mangen, Vern L. Bengtson, and Pierre H. Landry, Jr.
93. **Feminist Perspectives on Wife Abuse**
Kersti Yllö and Michele Bograd
94. **Common Problems/Proper Solutions**
J. Scott Long
95. **Falling from the Faith**
David G. Bromley
96. **Biosocial Perspectives on the Family**
Erik E. Filsinger
97. **Measuring the Information Society**
Frederick Williams
98. **Behavior Therapy and Religion**
William R. Miller and John E. Martin
99. **Daily Life in Later Life**
Karen Altergott
100. **Lasting Effects of Child Sexual Abuse**
Gail Elizabeth Wyatt and Gloria Johnson Powell

BEHAVIOR THERAPY AND RELIGION

Integrating Spiritual and Behavioral Approaches to Change

Edited by

William R. Miller
John E. Martin

SAGE PUBLICATIONS
The Publishers of Professional Social Science
Newbury Park   Beverly Hills   London   New Delhi

For information address:

SAGE Publications, Inc.
2111 West Hillcrest Drive
Newbury Park, California 91320

SAGE Publications Inc.   SAGE Publications Ltd.
275 South Beverly Drive   28 Banner Street
Beverly Hills   London EC1Y 8QE
California 90212   England

SAGE PUBLICATIONS India Pvt. Ltd.
M-32 Market
Greater Kailash I
New Delhi 110 048 India

Printed in the United States of America

Library of Congress Cataloging-in-Publication Data

Main entry under title:

Behavior therapy and religion : integrating spiritual and behavioral
   approaches to change / [edited] by William R. Miller and John E.
   Martin.
      p. cm. — (Sage focus editions ; v. 98)
   Bibliography: p.
   ISBN 0-8039-3203-0   ISBN 0-8039-3204-9 (pbk.)
   1. Behavior therapy. 2. Spirituality. I. Miller, William R.
II. Martin, John E., 1947-
RC489.B4B43513 1988   87-31954
616.89'142—dc19   CIP

FIRST PRINTING 1988

Contents

Preface 7

Acknowledgments 11

1. Spirituality and Behavioral Psychology:
   Toward Integration
   William R. Miller and John E. Martin 13

2. Three Contributions of a Spiritual Perspective
   to Psychotherapy and Behavior Change
   Allen E. Bergin 25

3. Integrating Behavioral Theory and
   Training with Personal Faith
   Paul W. Clement 37

4. Including Clients' Spiritual Perspectives
   in Cognitive-Behavior Therapy
   William R. Miller 43

5. Spiritual Dimensions of Health Psychology
   John E. Martin and Charles R. Carlson 57

6. The Relationship Between a
   Personal Theology and Chronic Pain
   Ellie T. Sturgis 111

7. Gaining Control by Giving Up Control:
   Strategies for Coping with Powerlessness
   James R. Baugh 125

8. A Religious Critique of Behavior Therapy
   Stanton L. Jones 139

9. Behavioral Psychology and Religion:
   A Cosmological Analysis
   E. Mansell Pattison 171

About the Contributors 187

With gratitude for the grace of our Lord Jesus Christ, and for all of our colleagues who are seeking their own integrations of the spiritual and psychological dimensions of life

Preface

In 1984, we embarked on an unusual task. We invited a group of behavior therapists to reflect on the integration of spiritual and behavioral approaches to change, and to present their reflections in a symposium at the annual meeting of the Association for Advancement of Behavior Therapy (AABT). The panelists, rising to the challenge, took up remarkably diverse aspects of this interface: faith issues in the training of behavioral clinicians, spiritual aspects of pain and suffering, the phenomenon of surrender and giving up perceived control, the compatibility of spirituality and cognitive-behavior therapy.

The response was surprising and encouraging. Scheduled at one of the least attractive hours, the symposium nevertheless drew a large and enthusiastic audience. We continue to receive letters and comments from those who attended, or who wanted to attend but could not, expressing their pleasure that this subject had at last been opened up. One result of the symposium was the formation within AABT of a Special Interest Group on Spiritual and Religious Issues in Behavior Change. Beginning from a list circulated through the symposium audience, the group has experienced a rapid growth in membership. A newsletter is now published semiannually, and the group meets at the annual meeting of the AABT.

The symposium was a beginning. A few seeds were planted, which, we hope, will continue to grow. Our immediate goal in this volume is to continue the dialogue on the ways in which spiritual and behavioral perspectives can be integrated and can enrich each other. To date, these two perspectives have developed in relative isolation from one another. Behavioral approaches have seldom been employed to understand or enhance spirituality, and spiritual or religious concerns are seldom considered in the teaching, clinical work, writings, or training of

7

behavior therapists. The reasons for this isolation are more historical than substantive, we believe, and we are encouraged at a few emerging signs of a new dialogue.

Even so, this volume makes us a little nervous. As behavioral scientists, both of us were trained to turn a skeptical eye on *mentalism* and experiential constructs difficult to observe or operationalize. For the most part, our research and teaching careers have been devoted to the development and evaluation of behavioral methods for change. Now here we are, editing a volume that discusses self, ego, acceptance, forgiveness, surrender, and yes, even God. At the same time, we fret at the difficulty of writing about and capturing the richness of spiritual life that we see in our clients and experience in ourselves. Nevertheless, we have forged ahead, with the potential critiques from both spiritual and behavioral colleagues already running rampant through our imaginations.

A beginning step toward integration is desegregation. Spiritual and behavioral perspectives have been kept far apart, dwelling and relating within their own constrained communities with very little commerce between them. Our hope in this volume is to hasten and encourage the process of desegregation, to give permission and occasion for meeting and dialogue. Sometimes the interface seems a bit forced—the interdisciplinary equivalent of mandated busing. Sometimes the touch points are natural, where the communities share common streets. We have sought, in the opportunity afforded by this volume, to invite a variety of exchanges across these boundaries.

The result is the somewhat unlikely concatenation of chapters that follows. Each touches on a different interface of behavioral and spiritual approaches to change. Each addresses issues of importance in themselves. Yet as you read these contributions, we recommend that you also look for the themes and commonalities that run through them. This is, in a way, the same process that we envision as optimal for integrating spiritual and behavioral approaches to change. Each has its own unique value, but in seeking their common essence, one may be led to discoveries not easily found within either alone.

We like here the illustration of the botanist, the butterfly, and the bee. The butterfly flits from flower to flower, touching the surface of each and tasting superficially. The botanist pulls flowers from their natural habitat to dissect and study them under the artificial light of a microscope. The bee, by contrast, goes to the heart of each flower, leaving it in its natural setting, extracting its pollen essence, and in the process cross-pollinating wherever it visits. The bee is fed. The flowers benefit, too. And then there arises a rich, unlikely sweet nutriment—honey. It comes only of the intimate interaction of bee and flower, and proves a delicacy to all who taste of it.

—William R. Miller
—John E. Martin

Acknowledgments

I would like to extend my gratitude to certain special individuals who have played important roles in my life, both spiritually and intellectually, over the past three years, and particularly during the time from the inception of the symposium planning to the eventual culmination of the final product represented here, including Charlie and Cindy Carlson, Keith Tonkel, Jim and Virginia Hughes, Ellie Sturgis, Stan and Brenna Jones, Jim Fitterling, Phil Godding, Carl Thoresen, John Fantuzzo, Al Litrownik, Sallie Strickland, Jim Hurley, Bill and Susan Richter, Jerry Fowler, Lamar Pace, Cindy Christian, Cheryl Lowe, Bebe Alexander, and, my brother, David Martin. I am particularly grateful to Rebecca Black, Gayle and Paul Soverign, and Joe Ozawa, and all the folks at Wells United Methodist Church in Jackson, Mississippi, and Mt. Soledad Presbyterian Church in San Diego, for their wonderful prayer support during the trial times when the book preparations ground to a halt or encountered seemingly insurmountable obstacles. Along these lines, I especially want to thank Rebecca A. Martin for her unwavering intellectual, emotional, and spiritual encouragement. Finally, I am deeply indebted to my colleague, coeditor, and friend, Bill Miller, who helped instrumentally in making this book a reality.

—JEM

I am grateful for the many students, colleagues, and friends who have joined and have encouraged me in the search for an integration of spiritual and psychological approaches to change. I have particularly enjoyed and appreciated John Martin's collaboration and companionship, which led to the creation of the Special Interest Group on Spiritual and Religious Issues in Behavior Change. This volume is but one result of that group's formation, and I look forward eagerly to seeing what other fruits will emerge.

—WRM

1

Spirituality and Behavioral Psychology

Toward Integration

WILLIAM R. MILLER
JOHN E. MARTIN

Historical Perspectives

Interest in spiritual aspects of human nature and development has a long and honorable history within psychology and psychiatry. William James, often called "the father of psychology" devoted an entire book to the subject of religious experience (James, 1902). Important figures in the history of psychology and psychiatry have been significantly influenced by religion and seminary education, among them Carl Rogers, Rollo May, Karl Menninger, and O. Hobart Mowrer. Major personality theorists have recognized the central importance of spiritual and religious aspects in human development and values: Carl Jung, Gordon Allport, Erik Eriksen, Viktor Frankl, Lois Barclay Murphy, Lawrence Kohlberg, Erich Fromm. Psychologists such as Paul Pruyser, Howard Clinebell, and Wayne Oates have devoted most of their professional careers to the field of pastoral counseling, and thereby have had major influences upon it. The psychology of religion seems to be experiencing a resurgence, and attracting new talent. The popularity of Scott Peck's books (1978, 1983) bespeaks an enduring public interest in the integration of psychology and spirituality.

What seems remarkable to us, however, is the almost total absence of significant contributions in this area from *behavioral* psychologists and psychiatrists. With a few exceptions (some of whom are represented in this volume), behaviorally oriented professionals have shown surprisingly little interest in things spiritual. The field of pastoral counseling has been molded in major ways by psychoanalytic, humanistic, and existential viewpoints, but until very recently there has been not a trace of behavior therapy in texts for pastors (Collins, 1980; Miller & Jackson, 1985). The theoretical and empirical foundations of the psychology of religion have only recently begun to draw upon the resources of behavioral psychology (Spilka, Hood, & Gorsuch, 1985). Paul Clement (1978) has decried the active hostility of many modern psychology training programs toward religious values and issues. Owing in part, perhaps, to the strong value influence of Skinner and Watson, behavioral psychology appears (on the surface, at least) to be at best indifferent toward the spiritual dimensions of human experience.

Definitions

Before we set about the task of integrating spiritual and behavioral approaches to change, it would be useful to clarify what each of these approaches encompasses. We seek not a definitive, but rather an operational, specification of the approaches to be dealt with in this volume.

As a working definition, we propose that *spirituality* entails the acknowledgment of a transcendent being, power, or reality greater than ourselves. Psychologist Paul Pruyser (1976) has referred to this as "awareness of the Holy," borrowing from a concept previously elaborated by Rudolf Otto and Friedrich Schleiermacher. Furthermore, spirituality involves an attempt to align and conform one's own life (both covert and overt behavior) toward this higher power. This may or may not include involvement in organized religion, but does involve intentional efforts to be in contact and conformity with the Holy. Said another way, from a spiritual perspective, the individual or collective humanity is not the measure of all things, but instead ultimate concern is vested in a transcendent reality, a higher power, a spirit.

When we write of *behavioral* approaches in this volume, we refer to the content and profession of behavior therapy. Broadly defined, behavior therapy represents applied experimental psychology, the employment of established principles of learning, cognition, physiological, developmental, and social psychology to the analysis and alleviation of human problems. Historically, behavior therapy has embraced not only a knowledge base, but also a method: the scientific method. Problems are conceived as dependent variables, and the behavior therapist seeks to identify and apply efficacious independent variables in their modification. The "behavioral" approach we are discussing here, then, is a *methodological* behaviorism, emphasizing empirically grounded psychological technologies that can be employed within a broad range of philosophic and value perspectives. Although it is possible to reconcile spiritual language with a more constricted radical behaviorism (e.g., Hayes, 1984), our present interest is in integrating spirituality with behavioral psychology more broadly defined.

Mutual Benefits of an Integration

We believe that there are persuasive potential benefits to be derived from an integration of spiritual and behavioral approaches to change. In part these gains would be in the opening of new dialogue: encouraging spiritually oriented people to think more behaviorally, and behaviorally oriented people to be more open to spirituality. But what imaginable good could come of this?

Some Contributions from Behavioral Psychology

William James was well aware that behavioral scientists may bring unique and helpful perspectives to the understanding of religious experience. Contemporary behavioral psychology is characterized by tools and disciplines that may be uniquely helpful in clarifying aspects of spirituality. This is particularly true as behavior research and therapy have begun to incorporate and operationalize more experiential phenomena such as cognition and imagery. What *are* spiritual experiences and problems? How do these overlap with other phenomena that we understand somewhat better, and in what ways are they unique? What causes an individual to understand an experience as a spiritual one? What are the components or dimensions of a person's spiritual life, and how might one go about assessing spiritual health? In scientific terminology, this amounts to a search for spiritual *dependent* variables.

Once identified, such variables can be measured, studied, enhanced, or modified.

Religious traditions and spiritually oriented people also suggest that we are dealing with phenomena much more important and powerful than mere semantic labeling. The self-reports of people for centuries have pointed to influential agency aspects of spirituality. Unless these are to be dismissed without investigation, such reports suggest that we should be searching to understand spiritual *independent* variables as well: factors that bring about change in people's lives. How do these overlap with change agents already studied, and how are they unique? In what ways do spiritual factors affect emotion and behavior, social adjustment, psychological and physical health?

To be sure, this is an unaccustomed juxtaposition of concepts: *spiritual* dependent and independent variables! The secular behaviorist may scoff at this superstitious nonsense, while the pious may despair at an attempt to put the richness of spirit under the microscope. Yet we *are* suggesting that there is value in pushing past these stereotypic biases that have thus far discouraged productive dialogue. Behavioral science approaches have already proven very useful in elucidating other areas of complex human experience: anxiety, sexuality, depression, obsessions and compulsions, addictive behaviors, self-fulfilling prophecies, marital relationships, anger, stress, attribution, motivation, and self-control. Why, then, should it be inconceivable to apply behavioral perspectives in attempting to understand those experiences called religious or spiritual, which people tell us so shape and change their lives?

Some Benefits from
Behavioral Psychology

Would there be a real benefit for spiritually oriented people in this endeavor? It is a bit too early to say. Perhaps it would turn out like the psychology of humor: an interesting exercise, but not one that seems thus far to have contributed significantly to the quality of humor in our society. Or might the psychology of stress and anxiety provide a better analogy for the potential benefits? Within two decades, knowledge in this area has progressed from largely literary metaphors of anxiety to an understanding of separate and important response systems that were previously confused under the same label (e.g., Lang, 1969). This breakthrough has enabled the effective specification of experiences and problems called "anxiety" and "stress," and hence the development of self-control strategies that significantly affect major sources of human suffering and disability.

Even at this early stage, some likely benefits are evident. Those who seek to follow spiritual disciplines often report difficulties that a behavioral psychologist would label as compliance problems: not sticking with a regular schedule of prayer or meditation, always meaning to start a process of spiritual study or service but never quite getting around to it, starting a program of spiritual development but then backsliding. These are familiar problems to a behavior therapist, and ones for which there are good solutions. Relatively simple behavioral self-control techniques might be taught and applied to address common problems of adherence to spiritual disciplines.

Any religious or spiritual value system is likely to prescribe and proscribe certain behavior patterns. Those seeking to follow a chosen spiritual path, then, are faced with the same difficulty of which Paul complained in the first century: "I do not understand my own actions. For I do not do what I want, but I do the very thing I hate" (Romans 5:17, RSV). Behavior change *is* a speciality of behavioral psychology! Yet too often the benefits of behavioral change methods have been inaccessible because of a lack of translation into a form acceptable and understandable to spiritually oriented people. Heated debates polarizing science versus theology have served further to isolate these epistemologies, even though both behavioral and spiritual approaches can be characterized as *empirical*—that is, experience-based. Behavioral psychology may offer useful behavior change methods to those who seek to conform their lives to a spiritual ideal.

Relatedly, many common obstacles to spiritual growth turn out to be specifiable problems that can be effectively (and sometimes easily) treated with behavior therapies. Obsessions, phobias, depression, anger problems, stress, interpersonal skill deficits, addictive behaviors, pain, and lifestyle-related illnesses—any or all of these can interfere substantially with spiritual development. Personal and pastoral application of effective behavior change methods could thus contribute to the fullness and richness of individual and collective spiritual life.

Still another common complaint within spiritual and religious circles is of compartmentalization. The spiritual aspects of believers' lives are often separated from secular life, relegated to circumscribed times of worship or the practice of particular disciplines. A result of such fragmentation is that the spiritual and value aspects of the person may fail to inform and guide his or her conduct in daily life. Efforts to reconcile behavioral and spiritual domains may, therefore, enable individuals and communities to experience their own integration and wholeness, rather than segmenting their experience into spiritual and secular components. Too often at present the spiritual community appears threatened by, and consequently ignores or rejects, the empirical and useful findings of secular behavioral science. (This threat and rejection is mutual, to be sure, with behavioral scientists too often ignoring the historic truths and richness of the spiritual as "superstition" if not pathology.)

A good example of the potential in integration is the current incorporation of modern medical science within religious thought and practice. As medicine developed into an empirical science, its technologies gradually achieved acceptance as valid curative approaches to be integrated with spiritual aspects of healing. One result has been a strong popular movement toward holistic health (e.g., *American Health* magazine; Cousins, 1979; Pelletier, 1979). We believe that a similar reconciliation is possible between spirituality and the science of behavior. The hunger of the population for such integration is already apparent in the enthusiastic response to popular writings on the subject (e.g., Peck, 1978). A substantial benefit for individuals and faith communities could be a better merging of spiritual dimensions of life with the flow of daily behavior.

These are but a few of the more obvious potential gains, visible from the beginning of the road. A concerted journey toward integration would doubtless yield others that are at present well beyond our ken.

Some Benefits to Behavioral Psychology

It is often the case that, when a relationship is beneficial to one party, the other benefits mutually, perhaps even synergistically. No different is the interchange and union of behavioral psychology and spiritual pursuits. We believe that an integration of behavioral and spiritual approaches to change would also enrich behavioral psychology in important ways. Here are but a few that we might anticipate.

(1) Enlarging the scope of inquiry. As it has matured, behavior therapy has encompassed an ever larger range of domains for study and intervention. Once constrained to overtly observable phenomena, behavioral psychologists have successively embraced physiological, then cognitive, then subjective affective events (Wilson, 1982). Kanfer and Saslow (1969) and Lazarus (1976) have proposed very comprehen-

sive approaches to behavioral assessment, evaluating nearly every aspect of a target problem *except* spiritual dimensions. Lang (1969) contributed a much-used trichotomy of cognitive, behavioral, and physiological aspects of a problem. The addition of a fourth dimension, the spiritual domain, might significantly enhance and enrich the capacity of behavoral science to understand, predict, and modify such complex phenomena as alcoholism, anxiety, and depression.

(2) Stretching the science. Behavioral psychology has long proceeded apace, guided by a set of fundamental assumptions that are so much a part of the normal *modus operandi* that they are often unquestioned. Determinism, atomism, and reductionism remain implicit philosophic givens for much of behavior therapy and behavior analysis. The consideration, examination, and incorporation of spiritual and religious issues within the realm of behavioral science will necessarily stretch and test these assumptions. One approach to integration is to retain these assumptions and apply them as tools for the behavioral and semantic analysis of phenomena called "spiritual" (Hayes, 1984). Another is to reexamine the assumptions themselves and consider whether they are proper guidelines for future behavioral science. In Chapter 8, Stanton Jones discusses the differing philosophic bases of spiritual and behavioral approaches, considering whether these divergent fundamental assumptions could pose substantial or even insurmountable impediments to integration.

(3) Unlocking training. The training of behavioral psychologists could acknowledge, incorporate, and address the spiritual dimensions of people. One of the most frequently expressed comments that we have received from colleagues and students is of this kind: "My faith has always been important to me, but I felt I had to hide it or even be ashamed of it during my graduate training." The affirmation of "spiritual behavior" (at least) as a legitimate form of human expression and experience would enable us to train behavioral scientists more as whole people. It is ironic that physical scientists report much more interest in and practice of religion than do behavioral scientists. Although training in behavioral psychology has typically shunned any consideration of spiritual dimensions, half of practicing psychologists and psychotherapists profess belief in God, as do 90% of their clients (Bergin, 1980). The lack of consideration and integration of spiritual aspects is a major deficit in most training programs. Paul Clement comments on this training aspect in Chapter 3.

(4) Raising clinical issues. Greater openness in training would also

better prepare behavior therapists to work with the majority of their clients for whom religious beliefs are important if not central. There is nothing inherently incompatible about cognitive/behavior therapy and spiritual/religious beliefs. Clients need not be asked to forsake their personal religious beliefs in favor of the therapist's perspectives (nor vice versa). Neither do therapists need to abandon a scientific perspective to delve into spiritual dimensions of therapy. Integration is possible, and makes behavior therapy accessible to a much larger population. The inclusion of spiritual perspectives in therapy is addressed by Allen Bergin in Chapter 2.

Bergin also raises an issue too often overlooked: the values implicit in therapy. Are there circumstances under which the alleviation of guilt or psychological pain is not the right thing to do? To what extent does a therapist—either consciously or unknowingly—proselytize for his or her own belief system? In bringing about behavior change in an individual, what will the impact be on those around the client? The juxtaposition of therapeutic and spiritual considerations brings these questions sharply into focus, and forces us to confront them. In Chapter 9, Mansell Pattison, a behavioral psychiatrist, reflects on some of the larger philosophic and value themes that are encountered as religion and mental health issues are brought together.

(5) Improving effectiveness and accessibility of therapy. The inclusion of clients' spiritual perspectives in therapy may also improve the effectiveness of behavioral treatment. One of the most vexing challenges for contemporary behavior therapists is that of producing *lasting* change in clinical problems (Brownell, Marlatt, Lichtenstein, & Wilson, 1986; Christensen, Miller, & Muñoz, 1978; Marlatt & Gordon, 1985). It is conceivable that this common phenomenon of relapse could be attenuated by carefully integrating and embedding behavior change strategies within the faith systems and spiritual practices of clients. The only confirmatory experimental evidence on this issue at present has emerged from the programmatic research of Rebecca Propst (1980). It is a very reasonable hypothesis, however, that spiritually oriented clients would be more likely to enter into, continue, and comply with a change program that is consonant with their central values and beliefs (Miller, 1985a). This is already at least dimly recognized in current emphases on the importance of expectancy factors (faith) and "placebo" effects (Epstein, 1984; Haynes, Taylor, & Sackett, 1979; Miller, 1985b). Cognitive-behavioral interventions may have greater impact when they incorporate the client's own belief and imagery systems. In this and

other ways, spiritual dimensions may provide additional resources upon which to draw in pursuing change. In Chapter 4, William Miller discusses how spiritual perspectives can be integrated into cognitive-behavior therapy.

(6) Broadening perspectives. There are areas of human experience that, for many people, already have profound spiritual/religious overtones and dimensions. One of these surely is the domain of suffering, a phenomenon that extends far beyond the limits of physical pain. As behavioral psychologists venture further into the realm of health psychology, we will have an opportunity to explore spiritual aspects as both dependent and independent variables in etiology, treatment, rehabilitation, and prevention. John Martin and Charles Carlson in Chapter 5, and Ellie Sturgis in Chapter 6, explore the interface of spirituality and behavioral health psychology.

It is probable that a synthesis of spiritual and behavioral approaches to change would also yield some new concepts and methods in behavioral psychology. To draw on the language of Reinhold Niebuhr's (1943) familiar "serenity prayer," behavior therapists have focused strongly on the "courage to change the things which can be changed," but have usually ignored or sidestepped the other, equally valid half: "grace to accept with serenity the things that cannot be changed." Why should this be so? Is not acceptance a cognition that can be operationalized, taught, restructured? Perhaps we have something to learn of the wisdom, to which Niebuhr referred, of knowing the difference between what should be changed and what cannot.

How many enriching insights and methods might evolve from a meaningful integration of spiritual and behavioral approaches? Many, we believe. We have touched on but a few here, and the chapters that follow offer a more in-depth, even provocative framework for further refinements and developments. In Chapter 7, James Baugh explores the paradox of gaining control by giving up control.

If in this chapter and this book we have provided more questions than answers, we are satisfied. The marriage of behavioral and spiritual perspectives remains far in the future, and no engagement date has even been set; in fact, it is fair to say that they have barely begun dating. There are those who augur doom and disaster for any such union. We disagree. Behavioral psychology is now well established as a useful and effective perspective through which to pursue the gifts of understanding and change. These two gifts have also been sought from religion since the beginning of recorded history. Spiritual and behavioral approaches to change are richly diverse. One has its roots in oral and written tradition, arises from within the individual, and claims kinship to powers greater than ourselves. The other has recent roots in behavioral science, arises from the scientific method, and attempts to operationalize, predict, and control the variables that shape our lives. The diversity of these approaches need not be construed as competitive, as a vying struggle for allegiance to one of two mutually exclusive perspectives. In their differing strengths, these two traditions show promise of melding. Until the process has progressed, the final properties and products of the resulting alloy can only be guessed.

Whatever they may be, we can be certain that they will transcend our early imaginings.

REFERENCES

Bergin, A. (1980). Psychotherapy and religious values. *Journal of Consulting and Clinical Psychology, 48*, 95-105.

Brownell, K. D., Marlatt, G. A., Lichtenstein, E., & Wilson, G. T. (1986). Understanding and preventing relapse. *American Psychologist, 41*, 765-782.

Christensen, A., Miller, W. R., & Muñoz, R. F. (1978). Paraprofessionals, partners, peers, paraphernalia, and print: Expanding mental health service delivery. *Professional Psychology, 9*, 249-270.

Clement, P. (1978). Getting religion. *APA Monitor, 9*(6), 2.

Collins, G. (1980). *Christian counseling.* Waco, TX: Word.

Cousins, N. (1979). *Anatomy of an illness as perceived by the patient: Reflections on healing and regeneration.* New York: Norton.

Epstein, L. H. (1984). The direct effects of compliance on health outcomes. *Health Psychology, 3*, 385-393.

Hayes, S. (1984). Making sense of spirituality. *Behaviorism, 12*(2), 99-110.

Haynes, R. B., Taylor, D. W., & Sackett, D. L. (Eds.). (1979). *Compliance in health care.* Baltimore, MD: Johns Hopkins Press.

James, W. (1902). *Varieties of religious experience: A study in human nature.* New York: Longmans, Green.

Kanfer, F. M., & Saslow, G. (1969). Behavioral diagnosis. In C. M. Franks (Ed.), *Behavior therapy: Appraisal and status.* New York: McGraw-Hill.

Lang, P. (1969). The mechanics of desensitization and the laboratory study of human fear. In C. M. Franks (Ed.), *Behavior therapy: Appraisal and status.* New York: McGraw-Hill.

Lazarus, A. A. (1976). *Multimodal behavior therapy.* New York: Springer.

Marlatt, G. A., & Gordon, J. R. (Eds.). (1985). *Relapse prevention: Maintenance strategies in the treatment of addictive behaviors.* New York: Guilford.

Miller, W. R. (1985a). Motivation for treatment: A review. *Psychological Bulletin, 98*, 84-107.

Miller, W. R. (1985b). *Living as if: How positive faith can change your life.* Philadelphia: Westminster.

Miller, W. R., & Jackson, K. A. (1985). *Practical psychology for pastors: Toward more effective counseling.* Englewood Cliffs, NJ: Prentice-Hall.

Niebuhr, R. (1943). *The serenity prayer.*

Peck, M. S. (1978). *The road less traveled.* New York: Simon & Schuster.

Peck, M. S. (1983). *People of the lie: The hope for healing human evil.* New York: Simon & Schuster.

Pelletier, K. R. (1979). *Holistic medicine.* New York: Delta/Seymour Lawrence.

Propst, R. (1980). The comparative efficacy of religious and nonreligious imagery for the treatment of mild depression in religious individuals. *Cognitive Therapy and Research, 4,* 167-178.

Pruyser, P. (1976). *The minister as diagnostician.* Philadelphia: Westminster.

Spilka, B., Hood, R. W., & Gorsuch, R. L. (1985). *The psychology of religion: An empirical approach.* Englewood Cliffs, NJ: Prentice-Hall.

Wilson, G. T. (1982). Psychotherapy process and procedures: The behavioral mandate. *Behavior Therapy, 13,* 291-312.

2

Three Contributions of a Spiritual Perspective to Psychotherapy and Behavior Change

ALLEN E. BERGIN

The behavioral movement, of which behavior therapy is one aspect, was established upon a foundation of conceptual building blocks that may be described as *mechanistic, naturalistic,* and *humanistic.* These were adopted for good historical reasons (Boring, 1950), and for many years they provided a structure and a stimulus for much good work that probably would not otherwise have occurred (see Skinner, 1953; Wolpe, 1958).

Gradual changes have, however, taken place that have required stretching these conceptual foundations. We now find ourselves dealing with a level of complexity and internal nuance that is beyond the elementary notions of stimulus and response. Social, affective, and cognitive variables have consequently been invoked as explanatory tools (Bandura, 1986; Mischel, 1986), and, as a result, the mechanistic-naturalistic-humanistic framework has given way to cognitive and agentive perspectives.

AUTHOR'S NOTE: This chapter, with the title "Three Contributions of a Spiritual Perspective to Counseling, Psychotherapy and Behavior Change," is forthcoming in *Counseling and Values*, published by AACD, © by AACD; used by permission. Originally, this chapter was delivered in a symposium on spiritual change and behavior change at the 1984 Annual Convention of the Association for the Advancement of Behavior Therapy in Philadelphia. Send reprint requests to Allen E. Bergin, 1120 SWKT-BYU, Provo, UT 84602.

There has, therefore, arisen a paradigmatic crisis—a competition for belief in the psychological community—between mechanical models and agentive ones. Professional values are being shaken in the process, and the shifting theoretical structure has opened the naturalistic philosophical monolith to the intrusion of spiritual factors that go beyond even the cognitive-agentive ones (Bergin, 1980a, 1983; Collins, 1977; Spilka, Hood, & Gorsuch, 1985). People like myself have waited a long time for this to happen, and now a rush is occurring to fill the vacuum left in our conceptual structure, as was manifested in the 1984 AABT symposium on spiritual change processes of which this article was a part. This does not mean to me entirely abandoning the former structure but building upon it by adding another cornerstone.

A cogent argument needs to be given for launching in this direction rather than mindlessly reverting to medieval notions of what the "spiritual" entails. There is, therefore, a growing substantive literature, which is interdisciplinary in nature, that addresses these matters. A full narration of arguments and evidences is beyond the scope of this chapter; but three implications for psychotherapy and behavior therapy that are of immediate importance are described in what follows.

In this context, it is important to recognize that a movement is occurring. It is not simply local within AABT or APA—it is a widespread cultural phenomenon, a kind of return to the study of values including spiritual values, but it is happening with new sophistication and more systematic and empirical analysis (Bergin, 1986). This trend is happening in various parts of the world (Gomez & Currea, 1983) and is not confined only to Judeo-Christian nations or traditions. Many new organizations and new journals have been formed. This movement did not begin at one point in time but it began to gather momentum in the early 1970s and may eventually reach the point of becoming an orientation (Bergin, 1980). The 1984 AABT symposium was, therefore, very timely and perhaps representative of trends yet to come.

In what follows, I put my own template on what is happening and describe it from the personal perspective of one participant. My template can be divided into three areas in which a spiritual perspective contributes to psychological thought and practice. One is a conception of human nature; the second is a moral frame of reference; and, the third, a set of techniques. The description of these contributions will be necessarily selective for the purposes of this brief account.

A Conception of Human Nature

With regard to theory, the most important notion is that there is a spiritual reality and that spiritual experiences make a difference in our behavior. This thesis is an essential centerpiece in a spiritual orientation, but it must be subjected to tests in the same manner that invisible realities in biology and physics are subjected to tests.

For instance, are verbal reports of religious experience correlated with important criterion variables, such as mental health? This question has been studied more thoroughly than most therapists are aware (see Bergin, 1983, for a review), and new studies are under way. We have been exploring the question of healthy and unhealthy religious experiences using a test battery and interview ratings. There is definitely a kind of religious experience that professional observers see as having healthy consequences as measured by usual observational methods (Bergin, Masters, & Richards, 1987; Bergin, Stinchfield, Gaskin, Masters, & Sullivan, 1988). These are similar to Allport's concept of intrinsic religiousness (Allport & Ross, 1967).

It is not necessary to be committed to a theory of spiritual realities to conduct such studies, nor are the results of the studies conclusive evidence of such phenomena. The self-reports do, however, provide a basis for making inferences about possibly powerful aspects of human nature that are unlikely to be inferred by means of other theories. Whether these inferences are more scientifically fertile than others remains to be evaluated via rigorous inquiry. Isaac Marks (1978) referred to this possibility after examining instances of dramatic behavior change consequent on religious experiences:

> When it works, faith healing has a power far surpassing existing psychotherapy technology. The order of magnitude of this difference is like that between nuclear and more conventional explosives. But we have not yet harnessed nuclear power satisfactorily, and our understanding of faith and religious processes is far more primitive than our knowledge of subatomic particles. Given a prepared mind, however, some paths into this labyrinth might be laid down. The important point is for hard-nosed experimenters to be alive to these possibilities, while retaining their methodological rigor. (Marks, 1978, p. 530)

Inferring the specific structures and processes involved in such phenomena is yet to be done; but the procedure is not different in principle from inferences made about invisible and indescribable "genes" in the history of biology or subatomic particles in the history of physics. Such concepts were enormously useful for a long time on the basis of indirect evidence before electron microscopes and other procedures made direct observation feasible.

Some of our colleagues are obviously enthused about these possibilities as is evidenced by the items in the reference list. Others are distressed by the prospect that such work could result in a regression to magical—or at least unscientific—thinking, a reversion to reliance on religious authority, or other dilutions of hard-won scientific progress (Ellis, 1980).

It is not necessary, however, to approach the spiritual in terms of traditional notions of the "supernatural." What is spiritual is different from ordinary matter, but it is still natural in that it proceeds according to laws. Assuming that there is such a thing as spiritual material or substance, it may be possible eventually to harmonize this viewpoint with empirical, behavioral, and materialist positions.

This suggests to me that what we refer to as spiritual experiences and spiritual realities are accessible, that they are not absolutely different from what we already know by the observation of the material world, and that the discoveries in the sciences of invisible but powerful realities have more similarity to the quest for the spiritual than the historical estrangement between science and religion suggests.

Our studies of people who report spiritual experiences appear to manifest connections between those experiences and the material world, such as in those behaviors that reflect mental status and life-style. We are also interested in their effects on physical health and whether there is anything beyond their relaxing effects, such as those noted in transcendental meditation. There is some evidence from Antonovsky's work (1979) that the sense of coherence in life that derives from spiritual convictions is correlated with physical health.

It is, of course, disturbing to try to embrace within the same frame of reference both mechanistic notions such as the existence of classically conditioned responses, and the idea that people have a mental apparatus with cognitive, agentive, and spiritual aspects. This is made much easier by assuming that the psychobehavioral aspects of organisms are multisystemic, just as the biological aspects are. Our bodies consist of semi-independent circulatory, nervous, muscular, skeletal, and other systems. These depend upon each other yet they also are entities unto themselves that follow very different laws—for example, the hydraulic laws of the circulatory system and the electrochemical laws of the nervous system. The laws of one system are not applicable to another system. If this is true for the body, it is likely to be true for one's psychology.

It is conceivable, then, that there is a system that functions according to classical conditioning that coexists alongside other systems having to do with agentive processes and spiritual processes, each having a part to play in the organic whole. Such "systems" are yet to be identified, differentiated, and described; but their possible existence makes it potentially feasible to harmonize seemingly incompatible perspectives as to how human beings function.

To me, the spiritual area is a rich source of hypotheses and intriguing problems for inquiry. While it remains to be seen whether a uniquely "spiritual" theoretical structure is needed to explain the phenomena being described in modern studies, whatever the outcome is, it should help us understand better the spiritual experiences that most human beings report and whether they are related to psychologically important behaviors.

A Moral Frame of Reference

The second important contribution of a spiritual perspective is that it anchors values in universal terms. This is important because therapeutic interventions are not value-free. Values determine the goals of treatment, the selection of techniques, and the evaluation of outcomes (London, 1986; Lowe, 1976).

What values determine the goals of treatment? How do we set those goals? All goals, whether they are goals for symptom relief or goals to modify a life-style are subtended by value systems. Elsewhere, I have argued that we generally seek to base our professional value decisions upon basic principles, and there I cited Hans Strupp's statement that major value themes seem to be universal (Bergin, 1985). This notion has been echoed by other people. Abraham Maslow, for example, was among the strongest advocates of such a view, in which he said, "Instead of cultural relativity, I'm implying that there are basic underlying human standards that are cross-cultural. Psychologists who advocate moral and cultural relativism are not coming to grips with the real problem" (cited in Goble, 1971, p. 92).

Ethical relativism is not consistent with the idea that there are laws of human behavior, nor with the specifically targeted goals of behavior modification (Kitchener, 1980). It is true that there is *cultural* relativism, that is, cultures differ and individuals differ in their values. But this does not mean that *ethical* relativism is true, that is, the notion that different ethics are equally valid or that different cultures are equally valid. Human growth, then, may be regulated in part by moral principles comparable in exactness with physical or biological laws, a position adeptly argued by Donald Campbell in his APA presidential address in 1975 (Campbell, 1976). Some writers, however, object to this thesis on the grounds that it has absolutistic tendencies. They say it is tainted by authoritarian, narrow, and judgmental frames of reference that are incompatible with the personal freedom that we prize and that we attempt to promote in our therapeutic interventions. The dichotomizing of lawfulness and freedom is oversimplified, however. Obedience to moral law is in principle no different from obedience to physical laws. We are free to launch a space shuttle into orbit only as we precisely obey the natural principles that make it possible. It may be that behavioral laws are just as precise, and obedience to them just as essential to obtaining desirable and predictable consequences. The freedom to self-actualize, for instance, is predicated on obedience to the laws by which self-actualization is possible. Thus the thinking that pits conformity to moral law (i.e., values) against individual freedom and then repudiates ethical universals may be inconsistent and misleading (Bergin, 1980b).

If we take seriously the probable existence of universals, as a large proportion of clinical thinkers do (Bergin, 1985), then the importance of guiding constructs for orienting choices and goals of clients becomes more evident. It appears that the laws pertinent to mental health should influence the way we construe the world, how we activate our agentive capacities, and the responsibilities we take for the way in which we act. Such patterns of cognitive evaluation and choosing we observe regularly in our clients as we discern the causes of their pain and suffering, as well as the changes that bring release and hope. Our awareness that certain principles underlie the processes of disturbance and therapeutic improvement anchors the way we think about therapy and the way we influence clients' views about how they might regulate their lives. This then provides them with cognitive structures (including values) for organizing the behavior being suggested by the therapist.

A good example of the application of the concept of universals is in the therapeutic attempt to promote self-control, a common practice in modern therapy. Enhancing self-control of impulses, addictions, or other nonadaptive habits is critical. Such self-regulation is enhanced by a belief that the regulation is valuable, that it leads to long-term consequences beneficial to the client and to those who are important to the client. In this respect, the therapist is in the role of a teacher or an instructor who is trying to help the client reconstrue the world and incorporate in the construct system values concerning intrapsychic and interpersonal consequences of behavior.

Endorsing such values and making them explicit helps both the therapist and the client realize that self-control can be guided in terms of possible universal themes. Self-discipline can never be optimally successful unless a commitment is made to values, and that commitment can be stronger and more lasting if the client feels that he or she is committing to something that is lawful and moral, not just because somebody said so but because it is built into the universe and is part of our nature.

While there is some disagreement about which values are relevant to mental health, there is a surprising degree of consensus concerning a number of values that are generally used to guide therapeutic efforts. My own informal survey of professional therapists identified 23 value statements about which there seemed to be considerable agreement (Bergin, 1985); and a subsequent national survey (Jensen & Bergin, in press) confirmed and extended these preliminary findings.

We developed a survey based on value-laden statements in the professional literature and administered it to a national sample of mental health professionals in clinical psychology, marriage and family therapy, psychiatry, and clinical social work. Responses were elicited from 67% of the psychologists, 64% of the social workers, 63% of the marriage and family therapists, and 40% of the psychiatrists. The values that mental health professionals endorse concern: (a) autonomy and responsibility, (b) perception and expression of feelings, (c) coping strategies, (d) physical health and fitness, (e) work satisfaction, (f) self-awareness and growth, (g) interpersonal skills and commitments, (h) marriage, family, and community involvement, (i) having a mature value system, and (j) responsible and fulfilling sexuality.

Some representative survey items considered mentally healthy, and the percentage out of 425 respondents agreeing to each item are as follows (high, medium, and low agree inclusive): "Assume responsibility for one's actions" (100%); "Develop effective strategies for coping with stress" (100%); "Develop the ability to give and receive affection" (100%); "Increase one's ability to be sensitive to others' feelings" (99%);

"Increase one's capacity for self-control" (99%); "Have a sense of purpose for living" (97%); "Be open, genuine and honest" (96%); "Find fulfillment or satisfaction in work" (97%); "Apply self-discipline in the use of alcohol, tobacco and drugs" (95%); "Acquire an awareness of inner potential and capacity to grow" (96%); "Be faithful to one's marriage partner" (91%); "Be committed to family needs and child-rearing" (90%); "Increase one's respect for human value and worth" (98%); "Be able to forgive parents or others who have inflicted disturbance in oneself" (93%); "Be able to forgive oneself for mistakes that have hurt others" (97%); "Understand that sexual impulses are a natural part of oneself" (100%); "Regard sexual relations as satisfying only when there is mutual consent of both partners" (94%).

There were many other specific items on these topics on which there was a surprising degree of agreement. There were also items on which the respondents divided. For example: "Have preference for a heterosexual sex relationship" (57% agree, 7% uncertain, 36% disagree); "Become self-sacrificing and unselfish" (52% agree, 9% uncertain, 39% disagree); "Have a religious affiliation in which one actively participates" (44% agree, 12% uncertain, 44% disagree). There was more division concerning specific spirituality/religiosity items than any other subgroup, but more general items elicited greater consensus, for example: "Seek a spiritual understanding of the universe and one's place in it" (68% agree, 9% uncertain, 23% disagree).

While a survey does not, by itself, prove that therapists have well-developed therapeutic value systems, it does indicate that they believe certain values to be relevant and helpful to mental health and treatment strategies. As far as spiritual values are concerned, there is a definite difference of opinion, as we found in a previous debate (Bergin, 1980a, 1980b; Ellis, 1980; Walls, 1980). Among the survey respondents and in the field generally, there are differences on specific moral issues, but there is also considerable consensus on values that appear to derive in a general way from the Judeo-Christian roots of our culture. To the extent that universals or "laws" are built into these values, as Strupp and Maslow suggested, they may form some elements of a therapeutic value system.

The importance of establishing a moral frame of reference is obvious to anyone who has carefully examined the value-laden nature of therapeutic interventions (London, 1986; Strupp & Hadley, 1977). To launch into the treatment of cases without a value perspective, as though such intervention is merely a technology applied to objectively defined disorders, is to invite disaster. A spiritual orientation reemphasizes the importance of being open, specific, and deliberate about values. It helps us shed our inhibitions about helping people activate values that can be used as cognitive guides in their self-regulation and life-styles. And it extends our values perspective beyond the narrow and immediate definition of good outcome we are accustomed to by emphasizing the broad, social, and long-term aspects that make life meaningful and life-styles fruitful, even across generations.

Techniques

The third contribution of a spiritual perspective constitutes a set of techniques (Collins, 1980). These range from intrapsychic methods, such as the use of prayer, scripture study, rituals, and inspirational counseling to family and social system methods that use group support, communication, mutual participation, communal spiritual experience, and group identification. We have already noted Marks's reference to faith healing. In addition, it is possible to utilize traditional spiritual involvements within standard therapy (Lovinger, 1984; Spero, 1985; Stern, 1985).

I will describe here just one illustration of a technique. I refer to it as the "transitional figure" technique, in which the client is taught to become a transitional person in the history of his or her family by first assessing his or her emotional genealogy. That is, the person is encouraged to see him- or herself as at a crossroads in his or her family history. As Erik Erikson put it, the case history is embedded in history, the history at least of one's family as it precedes and succeeds the individual.

The transitional figure, the client, is taught that though he or she has been the victim of pathologizing events in life, even though those events or persons caused a variety of pains and difficulties, that they must adopt a forgiving attitude. That is, the release of aggression against the victimizing agents, while it may be important at certain therapeutic junctures, is not healing in a deep and lasting way.

We introduce, in this context, the concepts of sacrifice and redemption that are common to great religions, especially the Judeo-Christian tradition. In this we are not referring to the extremes to which that concept has been taken but to the notion that the pain one is experiencing may have to be suffered in a certain way, that sometimes it is important to absorb the pain that has been handed down across generations. If your mother or father did it to you, do you necessarily blame them? Are there predecessors to their behaviors and to the behavior of those predecessors? Is it important, then, for somebody, sometime in the history of this pathological family to stop the process of transmitting pain from generation to generation? Instead of seeking retribution, one learns to absorb the pain, to be forgiving, to try to reconcile with forebears, and then become a generator of positive change in the next generation.

Some unusual changes have occurred in people who have adopted a role like this. One young woman had a bitter relationship with her father and expressed all of her negative feelings about him during therapy. The connections between his behavior and her problems seemed clear. After learning about the transitional figure idea, she was encouraged to go back to visit her father and, instead of confronting him with the pain he had caused, to invite him to tell her about his history and to do a family history interview. She was not to ask him about his dynamics or disturbances and their consequences but about his identity, experiences, and so forth. The result of doing this, including tape-recording and writing the interviews with her father, caused a dramatic reconciliation between them, a merging of perceptions of painful events that had occurred. It stimulated her father to face certain realities he had never faced. This was, however, a gentle experience occurring in a forgiving atmosphere. As a result, he was able to lower his defenses, apologize, and seek to make up for his past conduct. The changes in both client and father as a result of this encounter appeared to be dramatic and more profound than the changes that had been occurring via regular treatment (V. L. Brown, personal communication, October 1977).

As in religious tradition, sacrifice was required on the part of the client, that is, she gave up the need for retribution and separation from the past family network. And the sacrificial act, consisting of self-denial and forgiveness, yielded ultimate benefits to all parties that more than compensated for the sacrifice. Values guided this process that are rarely applied in psychotherapy but that have been part of major human traditions for centuries. A spiritual perspective reminds us that the development and endurance of such traditions is not likely to have been accidental or irrelevant to the needs of human beings (Campbell, 1976).

In conclusion, the spiritual template we have placed over the therapeutic enterprise shows the possibilities in that perspective for an alternative theory of human nature, for clarifying how values can facilitate change, and for the development of new techniques. This review provides but the simplest introduction to an important and growing literature. It represents an orientation that marks a decided turn in the interests and sympathies of behavioral scientists (Bergin, 1986); but it is one that can be harmonized with and is supportive of our vital and unchanging commitment to empirical science and to human welfare.

REFERENCES

Allport, G. W., & Ross, J. M. (1967). Personal religious orientation and prejudice. *Journal of Personality and Social Psychology, 5*, 432-443.

Antonovsky, A. (1979). *Health, stress, and coping.* San Francisco: Jossey-Bass.

Bandura, A. (1986). *Social foundations of thought and action: A social-cognitive theory.* Englewood Cliffs, NJ: Prentice-Hall.

Bergin, A. E. (1980a). Psychotherapy and religious values. *Journal of Consulting and Clinical Psychology, 48*, 95-105.

Bergin, A. E. (1980b). Religious and humanistic values: A reply to Ellis and Walls. *Journal of Consulting and Clinical Psychology, 48*, 642-645.

Bergin, A. E. (1983). Religiosity and mental health: A critical reevaluation and meta-analysis. *Professional Psychology, 14*, 170-184.

Bergin, A. E. (1985). Proposed values for guiding and evaluating counseling and psychotherapy. *Counseling and Values, 29*, 99-116.

Bergin, A. E. (1986). Psychotherapy and religious factors [Review of J. R. Lovinger's "Working with religious issues in therapy," and M. H. Spero's "Psychotherapy of the religious patient"]. *Contemporary Psychology, 31*, 85-87.

Bergin, A. E., Masters, K. S., & Richards, P. S. (1987). Religiousness and mental health reconsidered: A study of an intrinsically religious sample. *Journal of Counseling Psychology, 34*, 197-204.

Bergin, A. E., Stinchfield, R., Gaskin, T., Masters, K. S., & Sullivan, C. (1988). Religious lifestyles and mental health: An exploratory study. *Journal of Counseling Psychology, 35*, 91-98.

Boring, E. G. (1950). *A history of experimental psychology* (2nd ed.). New York: Appleton-Century-Crofts.

Campbell, D. T. (1976). On the conflicts between biological and social evolution and between psychology and moral tradition. *American Psychologist, 30*, 1103-1120.

Collins, G. R. (1977). *The rebuilding of psychology: An integration of psychology and Christianity.* Wheaton, IL: Tyndale.

Collins, G. R. (1980). *Christian counseling.* Waco, TX: Word.

Ellis, A. (1980). Psychotherapy and atheistic values: A response to A. E. Bergin's "Psychotherapy and religious values." *Journal of Consulting and Clinical Psychology, 48*, 635-639.

Goble, F. G. (1971). *The third force: The psychology of Abraham Maslow.* New York: Pocket Books.

Gomez, A. P., & Currea, F. B. (1983). *Psicoterapias 1983: Perspectivas de integration.* Bogotá, Colombia: Universidad de los Andes.

Jensen, J., & Bergin, A. E. (in press). Mental health values of professional therapists: A national interdisciplinary survey.

Kitchener, R. F. (1980). Ethical relativism and behavior therapy. *Journal of Consulting and Clinical Psychology, 48*, 1-7.

London, P. (1986). *The modes and morals of psychotherapy*. New York: Norton.

Lovinger, R. J. (1984). *Working with religious issues in therapy*. New York: Jason Aronson.

Lowe, C. M. (1976). *Value orientations in counseling and psychotherapy* (2nd ed.). Cranston, RI: Carroll Press.

Marks, I. M. (1978). Behavioral psychotherapy of adult neurosis. In S. L. Garfield and A. E. Bergin (Eds.), *Handbook of psychotherapy and behavior change*. New York: John Wiley.

Mischel, W. (1986). *Introduction to personality* (4th ed.). New York: Holt, Rinehart & Winston.

Skinner, B. F. (1953). *Science and human behavior*. New York: Free Press.

Spero, M. H. (Ed.). (1985). *Psychotherapy of the religious patient*. Springfield, IL: Charles C Thomas.

Spilka, B., Hood, R. W., & Gorsuch, R. L. (1985). *The psychology of religion: An empirical approach*. Englewood Cliffs, NJ: Prentice-Hall.

Stern, E. M. (Ed.). (1985). *Psychotherapy and the religiously committed patient*. New York: Haworth.

Strupp, H. H., & Hadley, S. M. (1977). A tripartite model of mental health and therapeutic outcomes. *American Psychologist, 32*, 187-196.

Walls, G. B. (1980). Values and psychotherapy: A comment on "Psychotherapy and religious values." *Journal of Consulting and Clinical Psychology, 48*, 640-641.

Wolpe, J. (1958). *Psychotherapy by reciprocal inhibition*. Stanford, CA: Stanford University Press.

3

Integrating Behavioral Theory and Training with Personal Faith

PAUL W. CLEMENT

The biggest roadblock to integrating two disciplines is the failure to have an articulated meta model for doing so. I suspect that most persons are not able to describe their own meta model for relating or comparing different philosophical perspectives and I believe that traditional disciplines don't contain a meta model for incorporating other disciplines. Each person and each discipline would benefit by having a clearly stated meta model. What is yours?

I would like to share four propositions that lie at the center of my own meta model. These propositions have facilitated the integration of empirical psychology and Christian faith in my own life and practice (see Carter & Narramore, 1979).

Disciples ≠ Disciplines

A *disciple* is a person who accepts and spreads the teachings of some other person(s). When such teachings stabilize and survive over a

AUTHOR'S NOTE: I thank the members of my research group for their comments on an earlier draft of this chapter, which was part of a symposium titled "Integrating Behavioral and Spiritual Approaches to Behavior Change," chaired by J. E. Martin and W. R. Miller at the 1984 annual meeting of the Association for Advancement of Behavior Therapy in Philadelphia. Requests for reprints should be sent to the author, The Psychological Center, Graduate School of Psychology, Fuller Theological Seminary, 180 N. Oakland Avenue, Pasadena, CA 91182.

significant period of time, they may become a recognized discipline.

Disciplines represent different ways of looking at the world. Each distinctive discipline represents a particular perspective that has developed, been articulated, and been shared by a large number of persons over decades or centuries. Examples of such disciplines are aesthetics, ethics, mathematics, psychology, and theology. Each has its own terminology, methodology, defined data base, and basic assumptions.

A discipline can be viewed as a complex set of *conceptual tools*. Depending on the problem facing a person at a given moment, the tools from one "chest" will be more relevant than those from the other chests. Over a lifetime, each person probably uses all disciplines.

A serious problem occurs, however, when the proponent of one discipline tries to explain away another discipline. For example, some disciples of psychology and theology have used each of these two perspectives in a competitive rather than a cooperative manner. Such competition can lead to an *intellectual imperialism* in which one discipline uses a radically reductionistic approach to capture the territory of the other. A good example of such an approach is John B. Watson's use of behavioral psychology as a replacement for religion (Watson, 1930/1970).

A solution to the above problem is to identify those disciplines or perspectives that are orthogonal and, hence, truly complementary. Orthogonal disciplines are like orthogonal measures within psychology (e.g., stable/unstable and introverted/extraverted, Eysenck & Rachman, 1965). First, they deal with different realms; therefore, information from one realm is not relevant for predicting into the other realm. Second, because they deal with different realms, using both perspectives provides more information than using either perspective alone.

Disciplines ≠ Data

In the beginning were the data; data preceded disciplines. Disciplines represent complex approaches to simplify and to make sense of the data. Although each discipline partially defines itself in terms of a realm of data, the data are not the discipline. Rather, the discipline is a set of assumptions about, terms for, and methods of dealing with the data.

At a given point in history, a given discipline is neither true nor false. It is simply more or less useful for solving certain kinds of problems relating to certain kinds of data. "Truth" can be a very troublesome concept. To the extent that "truth" has value, I assume that *data equal truth*. In contrast, because a discipline doesn't equal data, a discipline can't equal truth.

Furthermore, no discipline covers all the data of the universe. No discipline incorporates all perspectives on any one datum. No person can simultaneously use all perspectives; therefore, all understanding is only partial understanding (see I Corinthians 13:12). As indicated above, each independent discipline is ill-equipped to accommodate any other orthogonal perspective; therefore, each individual will need a meta model that can accommodate all of the philosophical perspectives used by that person to manipulate the data that are processed in a lifetime.

Data ≠ Meaning

Research articles in psychology and similar disciplines normally contain four primary sections: introduction, methods, results, and discussion (American Psychological Association, 1983). The results section focuses on the data, and the discussion section focuses on the meaning of the data. This editorial practice identifies the assumption that data do not equal meaning.

A given event (set of data) can be understood from many perspectives. Exercising different perspectives is dependent on processes that precede understanding. A simple story may illustrate the point:

[Speaker:] Did you know that Job spoke when he was a very small baby?

[Listener:] Where does it say that?

[Speaker:] It says, "Job cursed the day he was born." (Phillips, 1974, p. 2)

There are at least three levels at which this little story may be processed (see John 9): sensing, recognizing, and understanding. If you couldn't read the story, you couldn't recognize the words. If you couldn't recognize the words (for example, if you didn't know English), you couldn't understand the meaning of the story. But, you could recognize the words and still fail to get the joke. In such a circumstance, you understand the words but don't get the point of the story.

A common phenomenon that occurs when two disciplines encounter the same data is that, from the perspective of one discipline, the other doesn't get the real point of the data, that is, the other discipline doesn't get the joke. When persons of religious faith encounter behavioral psychologists who deny the spiritual dimension of life, they may accuse those "behaviorists" of not getting the point.

Meaning ≠ Methodology

Many contributors to the "behavioral movement" in psychology have behaved as though there is a necessary bond between philosophical and methodological behaviorism (e.g., Kantor, 1969; Skinner, 1953/1965; Watson, 1930/1970). Such a bond is not necessary; philosophical behaviorism does not equal methodological behaviorism. Defining observable behavior and environmental events as the data of an empirical/experimental psychology helped to make a science of human behavior possible, but creation of a science of human behavior did not speak to the meaning of life.

Unfortunately, many persons who actively used a spiritual perspective to interpret part of their observations rejected behavioral methods in the process of rejecting the philosophical premises of the developers of those methods. The misperception that behavioral methodology and spiritual concepts are incompatible has led to underutilization of behavioral psychology by religious persons and institutions (see Clement, 1981).

Fortunately, there is no necessary conflict between theology and clinical practice. Being right (e.g., claiming to have theological truth) does not equal might (e.g., knowing how to change behavior). Similarly, knowing how to change behavior does not equal knowing what to change or why. Combining theology and psychology to address a particular human problem has the potential for addressing what, why, and how simultaneously. The question is, Where do people do such a thing?

Graduate School of Psychology, Fuller Theological Seminary

The Graduate School of Psychology at Fuller Theological Seminary is such a place[1] (Clement & Warren, 1973). At Fuller, a student may relate disciplines, data, meanings, and methodologies within a doctoral program in clinical psychology. The program encompasses two disciplines (psychology and theology), two data bases (human behavior and the Bible), two perspectives (natural and supernatural), and two methodologies (empirical/experimental and inspirational/analytical).

The program exists for persons who want a setting that allows them to relate their psychology to their Christian faith. The theme of the program is "integration." Integration may involve *conceptual/theoretical* analyses (e.g., analyzing "forgiving" from a theological and a psychological perspective), *research* (e.g., performing an experimental analysis of the behavioral impact of the symbols used in corporate worship), *professional practice* (e.g., developing a day treatment program based on social learning theory and placing that program in a local church as part of its outreach ministry to the community), or resolving *personal questions or conflicts* (e.g., wrestling with questions such as "Who am I? Where did I come from? Where am I going? Who needs me? What do I want to do? Who cares? How do my psychology and Christian faith relate to each other in my daily living?").

Students in the Graduate School of Psychology spend at least six years full-time taking formal courses in psychology and theology; attending special lectures, workshops, and conventions that speak to the integration of these two disciplines; taking practica, traineeships, and internships that promote integration in professional practice; developing and refining methods and models of integration; doing empirical research and theoretical writing; and practicing professionally what they preach.

It is hoped that by the time they graduate they understand that they are different than the disciplines they use, their disciplines are different from the data studied, their data don't contain meaning, meaning is not methodology, and their behavioral methodology and Christian faith are complementary.

NOTE

1. Other institutions that offer doctoral programs that explicitly integrate psychology and Christian theology are at the Rosemead School of Psychology, Biola University, and Western Conservative Baptist Seminary.

REFERENCES

American Psychological Association. (1983). *Publication manual of the American Psychological Association* (3rd ed.). Washington, DC: Author.

Carter, J. D., & Narramore, B. (1979). *The integration of psychology and theology: An introduction.* Grand Rapids, MI: Zondervan.

Clement, P. W. (1981). Behavior modification of the spirit. In J. R. Fleck & J. D. Carter (Eds.), *Psychology and Christianity: Integrative readings* (pp. 112-120). Nashville: Abingdon.

Clement, P. W., & Warren, N. C. (1973). Can religion and psychotherapy be happily married? In R. H. Cox (Ed.), *Religious systems and psychotherapy* (pp. 417-426). Springfield, IL: Charles C Thomas.

Eysenck, H. J., & Rachman, S. (1965). *The causes and cures of neurosis.* San Diego, CA: Robert R. Knapp.

Kantor, J. R. (1969). *The scientific evolution of psychology* (Vol. 2). Chicago: Principia Press.

Phillips, B. (1974). *More good clean jokes.* Irvine, CA: Harvest House.

Skinner, B. F. (1965). *Science and human behavior.* New York: Free Press. (Original work published 1953)

Watson, (1970). *Behaviorism.* New York: Norton. (Original work published 1930)

4

Including Clients' Spiritual Perspectives in Cognitive-Behavior Therapy

WILLIAM R. MILLER

Mansell Pattison has observed that although pastoral and healing roles overlap heavily and share a common history, these functions have become widely separated in modern American society. "Priests and physicians grew too far apart. It left a large bulk of suffering persons with no adequate healers" (Pattison, 1978, p. 20). The alienation of psychotherapy from spiritual perspectives does indeed pose a quandary for religious people suffering from psychological problems. They may be reluctant to seek the aid of a secular psychologist, and not without reason. Psychologists are typically prepared, by disposition and training, to view all but the most watered-down religion as pathogenic (Clement, 1978; Ellis, 1980). The immediate alternatives may be parochial counselors with too little professional preparation in behavioral science and in treatment methodologies likely to alleviate the suffering. The religious client, then, is often left with a conflictual choice between a competent therapist hostile to cherished beliefs, or a like-minded counselor with less of the needed therapeutic expertise.

The gap has been particularly wide in the area of behavior therapy. Whereas both psychoanalytic perspectives and client-centered human-

AUTHOR'S NOTE: Portions of this chapter were presented as part of the symposium, "Integrating Behavioral and Spiritual Approaches to Change," at the annual meeting of the Association for Advancement of Behavior Therapy, Philadelphia, November 1984.

istic approaches have been well integrated into pastoral counseling, there have until recently been few efforts to synthesize spiritual with behavioral perspectives, and to integrate effective behavior therapy techniques into the mainstream of pastoral counseling (Bolin & Goldberg, 1979; Carter & Narramore, 1979; Collins, 1980; Miller & Jackson, 1985).

If such an integration is to begin, the cognitive-behavior therapies would seem a promising place to start. Both cognitive and religious perspectives are concerned with the implicit belief systems by which behavior is governed (Lawrence & Huber, 1982; Miller, 1985; Propst, 1980). Although the humanistic-atheistic values commonly attached to rational-emotive therapy may be antithetical to religious values, the *methods* of cognitive-behavior therapy can be extricated from Ellis's personal philosophy and applied in a more generalizable way (Wessler, 1984). This chapter is intended to be a contribution toward that extrication and application.

Arrogant Versus Collaborative Cognitive Therapy

Various differentiations have been proposed among the plethora of cognitive therapies that have emerged since 1970. Ellis (1979) has distinguished between "elegant" and "inelegant" forms of cognitive therapies, consigning Mahoney, Meichenbaum, Beck, Lazarus, and Franks to the inelegant category while identifying the elegant approach with Epictetus, Marcus Aurelius, and himself. At the risk of succumbing to such dichotomous thinking, I propose an alternative heuristic contrast between *arrogant* and *collaborative* cognitive therapies.

A central characteristic of the arrogant variety is the promulgation of a prescribed set of beliefs that are deemed "healthy," "rational," or otherwise desirable, in sharp contrast to a vilified list of "irrational," "unhealthy," or generally "stupid" beliefs that are presumed to be pathogenic. Once it is assumed that this right of discernment can be arrogated by the therapist, it then follows that therapy consists of a match-to-sample task in which the client is disabused of his or her mistaken beliefs in favor of the therapist's enlightened and superior views.

Ellis's crusading zeal in demolishing religious orthodoxy makes an easy target in this regard. Invoking scientific logic as his ultimate value, he maintains: "Since there is an exceptionally high probability that no gods or superhuman entities of any kind exist, we had better assume that they do not and live our lives according to this assumption" (Ellis, 1980, p. 635). (One must wonder how Ellis estimates such a probability!) Once this assumption is accepted, it is then logical to view a belief in any absolute as pathological, leading to his conclusion that "the elegant therapeutic solution to emotional problems is to be quite unreligious and have no degree of dogmatic faith that is unfounded or unfoundable in fact. . . . The less religious [people] are, the more emotionally healthy they will tend to be" (Ellis, 1980, p. 637).

Ellis has no corner on dogmatism, of course, and one can imagine any of a wide range of other orthodoxies against which client beliefs could be judged faulty. Fundamentalist religious counseling, for example, might be founded on the assumption that all psychological ills derive from insufficient appreciation of or adherence to certain dogmatic precepts. Exhortational counseling strategies then follow logically. The commonality in arrogant cognitive therapies is in their exclusive promotion of a prescribed set of beliefs as the one true road to health.

A more collaborative approach respects the integrity of the individual's belief system, and begins with exploration rather than renovation. The task is at once psychological and theological: to clarify the underlying rules that are governing the person's behavior. What are the individual's core beliefs, as reflected in behavior? What basic principles for living has the person derived from experience? Having clarified some of these basic assumptions, the next step is to help the client evaluate the *consequences* of accepting them, and to assess whether these are the consequences that the client desires or intends. Current behavior may be based on beliefs that once applied but no longer fit the client's situation. It is a process of bringing to awareness and evaluating the beliefs by which the person lives. Consideration can also be given to possible alternative assumptions and their consequences.

To be sure, this process is not value-free, nor can any therapy be (Bergin, 1980). An arrogant approach starts from a markedly different assumption, however: that the client's current beliefs are mistaken and must be exorcised. A collaborative approach, by contrast, acknowledges the therapist's values but also affirms the client's right to choose how to view reality. Exhortational or cognitive "search and destroy" tactics are rejected in favor of a joint explorative quest. Often, very beneficial cognitive restructuring can be accomplished without radically disrupting the client's basic system of values and beliefs.

TABLE 4.1
A Continuum of Dispositions in Cognitive-Behavior Therapy

Arrogant Assumptions	Collaborative Assumptions
Views therapy as a "match to sample" renovation of client beliefs	Views therapy as an exploration of beliefs and their consequences
Presumes to discern "healthy" or "rational" beliefs from "unhealthy" or "irrational" beliefs a priori	Evaluates consequences against client core values; compatible with diverse belief systems
Attempts to conform client beliefs to therapist assumptions	Attempts to modify client beliefs better to pursue the client's purpose and higher-order values
Emphasizes tangible proof or disproof of the truth of client beliefs	Client beliefs need not be overtly verifiable, though outcomes are
Reviles absolute, devout, or orthodox beliefs as pathogenic	Accepts and respects absolute core beliefs and values of the client

The arrogant/collaborative distinction actually represents more of a continuum than a dichotomy within cognitive-behavioral approaches. Table 4.1 states some characteristics of each extreme on this continuum.

Commonality and Divergence

A collaborative approach does retain some common assumptions of the cognitive therapies in general. One is that clients' belief systems are more than mere reflections of behavior, but rather they also play an executive role in governing behavior and affect. That is, holding a particular belief will result in certain behavioral, affective, and social consequences that differ from the consequences of an alternative belief. A second common assumption is that beliefs are modifiable and, consequently, that accepting new beliefs will result in altered behavior, emotions, and social impact.

Both arrogant and collaborative approaches share common *process* assumptions that are also underlying tenets of many religious systems:

(a) that beliefs are important determinants of behavior and emotional health, (b) that beliefs are modifiable, and (c) that accepting new beliefs results in altered behavior and emotion. The crucial divergence of these approaches concerns whether or not the individual's beliefs are directed by the therapist toward an a priori ideal standard. An arrogant approach is an ideological one, in which particular beliefs are prescribed as optimal while other are proscribed as pathogenic.

A collaborative approach invokes a somewhat more complex scenario: that individuals have a right to choose consciously the beliefs by which they will live. An informed choice of beliefs is enabled by many of the common processes of cognitive therapy (e.g., Beck, 1976; Burns, 1980): (a) discovering one's current *actual* underlying beliefs by inference from behavior, self-statements, and self-monitoring; (b) considering possible alternative belief and perceptual systems with which to view reality; (c) assessing and weighing the consequences of these alternative beliefs; (d) testing or trying out alternative belief systems; and (e) adopting (or retaining) a belief system that fosters the consequences (behaviors, emotions, relationships with others) that one desires.

A Case Example

Jon, a 24-year-old seminary student suffering from severe depression and anxiety, was referred by his pastor for psychological help. The pastor's diagnosis of depression seemed to be correct: his movements were slow and effortful, his posture was slumped, and he complained of a pervasive lack of energy. He had lost 15 pounds from his already thin frame and was suffering from insomnia, lying awake at night thinking self-critical thoughts.

Jon was the son of two missionaries widely acknowledged as models of unselfish giving. On his sixteenth birthday, they had given him a Bible inscribed, "Of him to whom much has been given, much will be required." He had been working incessantly, driven by an intense desire to serve others. My initial suggestion that he might back off a little and take some time for himself was met with the objection that he could not give in to "selfishness" and that the needs of others must always come before his own. He talked about relaxation as sinful, wasteful, and self-indulgent.

I saw him 11 times over the course of six months. He impressed me as a bright, energetic, well-intentioned young man with considerable potential for helping others. My initial plan was to work with him to reduce his apparent anxiety and depression by teaching him progressive deep-muscle relaxation (Rosen, 1977) and planning an increase in pleasant events in his daily life (Lewinsohn, Sullivan, & Grosscup, 1980). Both suggestions met with immediate strong objection, however, because Jon perceived both relaxation and "self-indulgence" to be inconsistent with his purpose in life, as he understood it.

My goal then became to work within his basic belief system, but to help him reevaluate the absoluteness of his self-imposed rules so that he might more effectively pursue what he understood to be his life purpose.

Our first few weeks of work together focused on cognitive restructuring. Jon kept a three-column diary recording *situations* in which he experienced a significant affect, the *self-statements* that occurred in these settings, and his resulting *emotions* and reactions. As he began to observe interrelationships among his self-statements and his emotional responses, several themes emerged that seemed to be frequent antecedents of depression. These centered on berating himself for personal shortcomings, thinking that he should be achieving and accomplishing more despite his fatigue, and believing that others were evaluating him negatively. These led us to three cognitive restructuring themes that proved to be acceptable and helpful to him. They are presented here in the order with which they emerged during therapy.

(1) Even servants have to rest and be restored. I asked Jon to consider whether by driving himself so relentlessly he was destroying his ability to serve. Service of the kind he expected of himself requires health and strength. I drew on biblical examples of how Jesus, his model, had taken times for rest, for solitary reflection, for visiting friends, and even, on occasion, for what his followers considered to be egregious self-indulgence (e.g., anointing with oil). These acts, I suggested, were not signs of weakness or selfishness, but rather wise and necessary times of re-creation for one who would give himself to a life of service.

(2) Grace. In his perfectionism, Jon complained that, "No matter how hard I work, it's never good enough." Here I invited him to reflect on whether he really believed the message of grace that he wished to carry to others: that human beings, though imperfect, can also be forgiven and accepted. In his personal theology, as it turned out, he understood grace as a free and unmerited gift, never earned but only received. I urged him to experience the meaning of this for himself first, if he wanted to get the message across to others. Furthermore, I suggested, he would need to

accept and fully experience this grace himself if he wished to share it with others.

(3) Focus on others. I pointed out that although Jon stated a desire to focus his life on others, he spent a good deal of time and energy focusing his concern on himself, worrying about his performance and how others were judging it. We discussed how he might use self-instruction when he found this happening, telling himself to focus his attention and interest on others instead of wasting his energies on anxious self-consciousness.

After several weeks of self-monitoring and discussion, Jon was prepared to begin trying some new strategies and to observe their consequences. We constructed several "replacement thoughts" to be used as new self-statements when he found himself engaged in self-talk of the varieties described above. These included the following:

(1) Even Jesus took time to rest and recharge.
(2) If I want to serve, I also need to take care of myself.
(3) God, through Jesus Christ, accepts me as I am.
(4) Don't worry about how other people are evaluating *me*. Focus on *their* needs instead.
(5) I have good news to share!

These alternative self-statements proved very acceptable to Jon, because they were consistent with and expressed important elements of his core belief system. Jon found that, when he began feeling distressed, he could usually identify an "old" self-statement. He further discovered that, by replacing it with one of the new statements we had devised, he could often alter his mood.

As this took effect, Jon became more amenable to considering the behavioral strategies I had proposed unsuccessfully at the outset. We began a course of relaxation training. I assigned him to practice this several times weekly, and further suggested that he concentrate on moving in a more relaxed and slow fashion, rather than rushing about as he had been wont to do. We also began to plan a few specific pleasant events for each week.

Using these methods of cognitive restructuring, self-instruction, relaxation, and pleasant events scheduling, Jon showed an encouraging reduction in his depression and anxiety. He began sleeping normally and regained about 10 pounds. Then in the ninth session, after a month's recess, Jon reported a recurrence of his symptoms. He indicated that he had stopped practicing relaxation and pleasant events, and had failed to use his cognitive strategies for almost three weeks, even though these strategies clearly had been working for him. I queried whether in some way he might be reluctant to give up his depression and anxiety. After some silent thought, he remarked, "It's my wooden leg! If I no longer have this impediment, then what will be expected of me?" I asked him to reflect between sessions on a question that Jesus sometimes asked: "Do you want to be healed?" and to practice regularly his self-statements regarding acceptance and grace. His "wooden leg" insight seemed to be an important step. Two sessions later, Jon was much improved, was again practicing his self-change strategies, and indicated that he felt able to go on alone. I remain in contact with him four years later, and he is continuing to function well, pursuing his chosen mission career and helping many others through his renewed energy.

Discussion

This case example is illustrative of a collaborative approach to cognitive-behavior therapy, incorporating the client's own spiritual perspectives into the healing process. Although spiritual dimensions have commonly been ignored in behavioral assessment and treatment, there are no impelling reasons why we as psychologists need to continue pretending that our clients' religious beliefs do not or should not exist. Spiritual dimensions can add to diagnostic understanding (Pruyser, 1976), and behavior therapies can readily be combined with procedures that explicitly invoke clients' religious and metaphysical beliefs (e.g., Benson & Proctor, 1984; Emmons, 1978; Miller, 1985).

Although religious beliefs themselves may not be subject to scientific verification, their psychological manifestations and applications in treatment *are* empirically testable. Propst (1980), in one of the first controlled outcome studies of this kind, found that depressed individuals with at least moderately high scores on a test of religiosity responded better to religious imagery therapy than to nonreligious imagery or self-monitoring alone. Whether the incorporation of theological constructs will amplify the effectiveness of cognitive-behavior therapies (at least for religious people) remains an open question. Even if it does not, however, such modification can render the ordinary documented benefits of such therapy available to a population that might otherwise shun this approach.

Religious beliefs may even find their way into behavioral theory. The recent renewal of interest in Skinner's (1969) concept of "rule-governed behavior" affords just such an opportunity. The concept recognizes that individuals can abstract rules from their own experience, and that these rules may then supersede extant contingencies. Viewed from this perspective, many therapeutic systems (e.g., insight therapies, reality therapy, behavior therapies) can be seen as an attempt to bring the client's implicit rules into maximal correspondence with actual social contingencies. That is, a "functional" or "adjusted" person is understood to be one whose behavior-governing rules reflect genuine current contingencies. Because at least some religious beliefs precisely represent such behavior-governing rules, they can be incorporated into the theory.

Religious perspectives also introduce a metadimension that may enrich theoretical and ethical reflection. Bergin (1980) has criticized "clinical pragmatism" (of which he considers behavior therapy to be representative) for conforming clients to the status quo, to contingencies as they now exist. One value of spiritual perspectives is that they afford a perception of reality not only as it is, but as it could be. The history of saints and martyrs is a history of individuals who lived by rules that differed in important ways from the standard contingencies of their day. The collaborative cognitive therapy approach described here is one that utilizes the concept of rule-governed behavior, raising the client's awareness of rules and assumptions. It does *not*, however, inherently presume that it is desirable to alter the individual's rules to conform with the "reality" contingencies as understood by the therapist (the central premise of an arrogant approach).

What might be the effects of adopting behavior-governing rules that do not correspond to current contingencies? To be sure, some of the consequences are likely to be aversive and emotional. Yet social contingencies are not invariant, and it is quite conceivable that living as if different rules were in effect can alter contingencies in the direction of that belief (Jones, 1977; Miller, 1985). Widespread behavioral disregard of particular statutes, for example, has led to their repeal or alteration (e.g., alcohol prohibition). Civil rights activists of the 1960s effectively protested and altered racial segregation laws through behaviors that violated these rules. Cervantes's fictional knight, Don Quixote, transformed those around him by the very fact that his behavior was governed by rules that differed from their own reality. It is a psychological frontier worthy of further exploration: that consciously chosen behavior-governing rules are catalysts of both personal and social change. In consideration of such issues, the overlap between therapeutic and religious interests becomes great.

Because there is no foreordained doctrinal criterion for the client to match, a collaborative approach to cognitive therapy often opens up deeper explorations of the individual's core values. The suggestion is of a hierarchy of beliefs, among which a few are essential, definitive of the individual. Tillich (1957, p. 10) referred to this as a person's *ultimate concern*, "that which is really ultimate over against what claims to be ultimate but is only preliminary, transitory, finite." Tillich saw this "ultimate concern" as central to the whole personality, essential to understanding the person. For the individual, the clarification of ultimate concern is an explication of what is regarded as sacred: "What concerns one ultimately becomes holy" (Tillich, 1957, pp. 12-13; see Pruyser, 1976).

For Jon, a core value seemed to be his commitment to the service of others. His belief that relaxation is sinful subserved his ultimate concern for servanthood. When it became apparent to him, through collaborative cognitive therapy, that this secondary belief actually eventuated in consequences that undermined and disabled his primary purpose (as he understood it), he altered the secondary (Tillich would say "preliminary") belief and its related behavior toward consistency with his ultimate concern.

This is a potential new domain for cognitive assessment: the determination of belief hierarchies, and thereby of the most central or core values that define the individual. Such assessment will require sophisticated procedures, still to be developed, that may be hybrids of psychometrics and systematic ethics. It may be possible, too, to draw upon analogues from other disciplines to apply in exploring personal belief structures. The cybernetic concept of rule-based "expert systems," for example, might provide a formative paradigm for modeling belief hierarchies in individuals (Hayes-Roth, Waterman, & Lenat, 1983). Various assessment strategies also exist for clarifying personal belief systems (e.g., Hall & Ledig, 1986).

The clarification of a client's core values is an exploratory process that presses beyond the modification of troubling cognitions, and beyond match-to-sample cognitive restructuring. It evokes a meta-therapeutic dimension in which the individual's personal and essential beliefs are discovered (itself a potentially therapeutic endeavor) and then used as the reference point toward which other cognitive-behavioral interventions can be directed.

It would be pretentious and fallacious to presume that such therapeutic exploration could proceed unaffected by the therapist's own values. Carl Rogers's presumably "nondirective" approach was revealed, on careful analysis by his students, to in fact be selectively reinforcing certain beliefs and self-statements in the client (Truax, 1966). There is a hazard in this "collaborative" approach of pursuing the arrogance of restructuring client beliefs to resemble one's own, but doing so more subtly. The fact that self-statement modification is effective in modifying beliefs and behavior (Dush, Hirt, & Schroeder, 1983) is cause for concern regarding renovation of client beliefs in the guise of psychotherapy.

A hope for protection against this danger is the very explicitness of the collaborative restructuring process. The value dimensions are explicit, and indeed form a focus of the therapy. The client's current system of beliefs and assumptions is clarified, with a process of sorting to determine which seem most central or cherished. The consequences of these beliefs are explored, checking hypotheses against the client's own behavior and subjective experience. Alternative assumptions and perspectives are generated and evaluated. The client may be assigned to "try on" a new belief pattern for a week as a homework assignment, while self-monitoring relevant affective, behavioral, and cognitive consequences (see Kelley, 1955).

It may also be desirable for the therapist to acknowledge explicitly his or her own values and beliefs relevant to the areas being explored with the client. There are trade-offs here. In disclosing personal beliefs, the therapist may be implicitly modeling a "healthy" belief system and encouraging the client to adopt at least aspects of it. On the other hand, failure to acknowledge one's own perspectives may increase the likelihood of subtle persuasive biasing.

As a compromise, the therapist's personal values might be introduced with several caveats: (a) that the purpose of doing so is to acknowledge them openly, with the hope of *preventing* the client from merely adopting them; (b) that, in the therapist's view, there is no universal and absolute ideal or healthy set of beliefs, but rather each person adopts and evaluates values based on personal experience. In an explicit sharing of belief systems, of course, it is possible that either therapist or client may decide that there is too great a discrepancy in values for a therapeutic relationship to proceed.

The essential point I have wished to make here is that it is feasible to guide cognitive-behavior therapy toward ends derived from the client's own core values, rather than toward a single preconceived notion of which beliefs are "rational" and which "irrational." The cognitive-behavior therapist can honor the client's own core values, moving therapy in a direction consonant with the individual's faith system. Both by respecting the integrity of the client's beliefs and by clarifying (as explicitly as possible) the essential values being pursued and served, a collaborative cognitive-behavioral approach can be compatible with and facilitative of the spiritual dimensions of change.

REFERENCES

Beck, A. T. (1976). *Cognitive therapy and the emotional disorders.* New York: International Universities Press.

Benson, H., & Proctor, W. (1984). *Beyond the relaxation response.* New York: Times Books.

Bergin, A. E. (1980). Psychotherapy and religious values. *Journal of Consulting and Clinical Psychology, 48,* 95-105.

Bolin, E. P., & Goldberg, G. M. (1979). Behavioral psychology and the Bible: General and specific considerations. *Journal of Psychology and Theology, 7,* 167-175.

Burns, D. D. (1980). *Feeling good: The new mood therapy.* New York: Morrow.

Carter, J. D., & Narramore, B. (1979). *The integration of psychology and theology.* Grand Rapids, MI: Zondervan.

Clement, P. W. (1978). Getting religion. *APA Monitor, 9*(6), 2.

Collins, G. (1980). *Christian counseling.* Waco, TX: Word.

Dush, D. M., Hirt, M. L., & Schroeder, H. (1983). Self-statement modification with adults: A meta-analysis. *Psychological Bulletin, 94,* 408-422.

Ellis, A. (1979). Rational-emotive therapy as a new theory of personality and therapy. In A. Ellis & J. Whiteley (Eds.), *Theoretical and empirical foundations of rational emotive therapy* (pp. 1-6). Monterey, CA: Brooks/Cole.

Ellis, A. (1980). Psychotherapy and atheistic values: A response to A. E. Bergin's "Psychotherapy and religious values." *Journal of Consulting and Clinical Psychology, 48,* 635-639.

Emmons, M. L. (1978) *The inner source: A guide to meditative therapy.* San Luis Obispo, CA: Impact.

Hall, B. P., & Ledig, B. D. (1986). *Manual for the Hall-Tonna Inventory of Values.* Palo Alto, CA: Behaviordyne.

Hayes-Roth, F., Waterman, D., & Lenat, D. (1983). *Building expert systems.* Reading, MA: Addison-Wesley.

Jones, R. L. (1977). *Self-fulfilling prophecies: Social, psychological, and physiological effects of expectancies.* New York: Lawrence Erlbaum.

Kelley, G. A. (1955). *The psychology of personal constructs.* New York: Norton.

Lawrence, C., & Huber, C. H. (1982). Strange bedfellows? Rational-emotive therapy and pastoral counseling. *Personnel and Guidance Journal, 61,* 210-212.

Lewinsohn, P. M., Sullivan, M. J., & Grosscup, S. J. (1980). Changing reinforcing events: An approach to the treatment of depression. *Psychotherapy: Theory, Research, and Practice, 17*, 322-334.

Miller, W. R. (1985). *Living as if: How positive faith can change your life.* Philadelphia: Westminster.

Miller, W. R., & Jackson, K. A. (1985). *Practical psychology for pastors: Toward more effective counseling.* Englewood Cliffs, NJ: Prentice-Hall.

Pattison, E. M. (1978). Psychiatry and religion circa 1978: Analysis of a decade, Part I. *Pastoral Psychology, 27*, 8-25.

Propst, L. R. (1980). A comparison of the cognitive restructuring psychotherapy paradigm and several spiritual approaches to mental health. *Journal of Psychology and Theology, 8*, 107-114.

Pruyser, P. W. (1976). *The minister as diagnostician.* Philadelphia: Westminster.

Rosen, G. M. (1977). *The relaxation book: An illustrated self-help program.* Englewood Cliffs, NJ: Prentice-Hall.

Skinner, B. F. (1969). *Contingencies of reinforcement.* New York: Appleton-Century-Crofts.

Tillich, P. (1957). *Dynamics of faith.* New York: Harper.

Truax, C. (1966). Reinforcement and nonreinforcement in Rogerian psychotherapy. *Journal of Abnormal Psychology, 71*, 417-422.

Wessler, R. L. (1984). A bridge too far: incompatibilities of rational-emotive therapy and pastoral counseling. *Personnel and Guidance Journal, 62*, 264-266.

5

Spiritual Dimensions of Health Psychology

JOHN E. MARTIN
CHARLES R. CARLSON

> If you listen carefully to the voice of the Lord your God and do what is right in his eyes, if you pay attention to his commands and keep all his decrees, I will not bring on you any of the diseases I brought on the Egyptians, for I am the Lord who heals you. (Exodus 15:26; NIV)

These words of God to the Hebrew people strongly point to both the health woes that accompany a life-style that is in disharmony with spiritual and Godly principles and to the contrasting healing power of God's favor. Although this statement would appear to the nonreligious scientist as reflecting historically inaccurate, scientifically unsound and untestable interpretations made by the religiously persuaded, and while believing Jews and Christians would be hard pressed to contend that *no* physical hardships or diseases would befall those who follow God's (scriptural) prescriptions and proscriptions for a spiritual way of life, there may be some good scientific reasons why modern behavioral

AUTHORS' NOTE: The authors would like to express their appreciation to Robert M. Kaplan for his suggestions that led to the inclusion of several bodies of supportive research to the present chapter, to Rebecca A. Martin for her careful reading and critique of the manuscript, to Cindy and Jeremiah Carlson and Stan and Brenna Jones for their love and unwavering support, to Al Litrownik for his professional support and encouragement, to Michelle Toshima for her reading of and helpful comments on the manuscript, and finally to Sallie Strickland and Ann Walker for their technical assistance during the preparation of the chapter.

scientists should take a much closer look. In fact, there is a growing body of evidence that spiritually oriented life-styles may be associated with reduced incidence of disease and health risk factors, as well as enhanced quality of life. Perhaps even more critically, the converse may also be true. The lack of adherence to spiritual dictates, principles, and prescribed life-styles may be associated with relatively poorer physical and emotional health—findings that we believe the scientific community can no longer afford to ignore. Similarly, we believe these investigations into the efficacy of spiritual and/or Godly life-styles are of great importance to the majority who are spiritual and/or religious, and that efforts to quantify, demonstrate, and differentiate better these phenomena should be greeted with trusting enthusiasm rather than spiritual and theological arrogance, or fearful avoidance. If, indeed, "all Truth [including science] is God's Truth," should it not be open to, as well as be able to withstand, scientifically objective, truth-seeking investigations and investigators? We believe so. Thus it is with these challenges in mind that we bring the following provocative body of literature to the reader's attention.

Rationale

William James, one of the earliest psychologists to attempt to integrate religion and psychology, wrote in his *The Varieties of Religious Experience* (1903) that faith can affect both physical health and disease processes. Since James first developed these hypotheses, there have been a number of findings, anecdotal and scientific, that support their credibility. The remainder of the chapter will, therefore, attempt to elucidate these most intriguing associations of spirituality, health, and disease, in order that clinicians and researchers interested in this area might have a better understanding of how to investigate these associations further, as well as adapt them within a therapeutic context, particularly with their spiritually oriented clients. As research clinical psychologists specializing in the area of health psychology and behavioral medicine, who value a spiritually oriented life-style, we have come to a growing awareness of the oftentimes disastrous effects of less- or non-spiritually oriented life-styles on physical health and overall quality of life.

As we pondered the development of this chapter, we decided to begin by defining two terms essential to the task at hand, which is to explore the boundary areas where spirituality and health psychology intersect.

We suspect the intersection of these two concerns will be an important area of inquiry within psychology during the coming years. In order to avoid misunderstanding, we must necessarily define our usage of the terms, *spirituality* and *health psychology*, at the outset.

Definition of *Spirituality*

Spirituality, as we see it, is a process by which individuals recognize the importance of orienting their lives to something nonmaterial that is beyond or larger than themselves (an ultimate reality, if you will), so that there is an acknowledgment of and at least some dependence upon a higher power, or Spirit. A spiritual person in our view does not believe that humankind is the measure of all things, but rather that humans are an incomplete reflection of what is perfect. In order to clarify better the cognitive and belief filters through which this chapter ultimately passed, it is important to note that our specific core beliefs posit spirituality as involving a personal process directed toward relating oneself to the ultimate higher power, God. An extension of this belief that many in our culture would include in their definition of *spiritual* is a central belief in God as an "invisible, personal, and living Spirit" (Lewis, 1984, p. 451) who is the creator of life and the perfect personage worthy of being sought out. While many would not go so far in this definition (in fact, only 50% of psychologists in APA believe in God at all; Bergin, 1980), the vast majority (over 80%-90%) of the American population do believe in God, with 31% of those considering themselves fundamental or "born-again" believers (Princeton Religion Research Center, 1986). Further, these figures do not merely represent the "ignorant" and the "truly needy" who do not know any better. For example, in a recent survey of Stanford University undergraduates, Rosenhan (1987) found that a majority (75%) of the respondents acknowledged a belief in God, while 65% of the total sample indicated they believed in an afterlife; 28% reported they believed in "miracles," with at least 15% of those questioned considering themselves "born-again" Christians. Overall, 56% of the Christians (presumably representing the majority of those professing a belief in God) related that they frequently or occasionally felt "close to the Divine" (Rosenhan, 1987).

Although we might have chosen a much broader definition of *spirituality* (e.g., "new age"), thus avoiding the scientifically controversial inclusion of God, this chapter will emphasize this more theistic definition of the spiritual person and way of life—though not to the exclusion of other forms of spirituality. We have committed ourselves to this conservative course—though this tact may be less acceptable to even our broadest-minded scientific colleagues—for two primary reasons: (a) to reflect a more classically accepted conception from the standpoint of the major religious meta-system in the Western world, the Judeo-Christian heritage; and (b) to provide a more exclusive, better-circumscribed framework from which to differentiate more-spiritual from less-spiritual orientations, systems, and/or life-styles—particularly those that may be more "earthbound" in their worldview and expression of beliefs (e.g., humanism). Spirituality from the standpoint of this definition is markedly different from a way of life based upon the belief that humans are the ultimate form of existence. Viewing "man as the measure of all things" is not compatible with a spiritual life-style as we are defining it. Spirituality, especially from the prevailing viewpoint of academic clinical psychology (see Bergin, 1980), stands in sharp contrast to a humanistic perspective (e.g., Ellis, 1971, 1980), which posits the centrality of human thought, knowledge, and power, and further suggests the operation of irrational, even pathological, belief systems when higher forms and orientations of life are valued and given consideration.

One may then ask, How do we distinguish this spiritual person? Several characteristics and practices would seem to make this differentiation. First, as noted above, the spiritual individual either ascribes to the core belief of a perfect God, who is the creator of all things, or to an ultimate reality, a Spirit that is not man-made or material. Second, this person likely (but not necessarily) engages in the regular practice of prayer, meditation, spiritual study, and/or worship of God, for the purpose of becoming more "Godly" or closer to the divine. Third, the individual makes heartfelt attempts to bring his or her own behavior and thinking in line with spiritual teachings (see Pattison, Chapter 9). Fourth, the spiritual person may pursue active spiritual and/or social practices and fellowship with other like-minded persons. Finally, the spiritual person's worldview, beliefs, thoughts, and behaviors rest importantly upon and are colored by his or her Faith—faith in the truth and value of his or her spiritual orientation in explaining and ordering the world, its events, and inhabitants. Thus when we speak of spirituality in this chapter, this is our understanding and usage. We recognize differing views exist; because there is room for misinterpretation, we have provided an outline of our core beliefs regarding spirituality at the outset of the chapter.

Definition of *Health Psychology*

Health psychology is also a phrase with many different meanings. Our use of the terms follows Matarazzo (1980, p. 815), who defined *health psychology* as "the aggregate of the specific educational, scientific, and professional contributions of the discipline of psychology to the promotion and maintenance of health, the prevention and treatment of illness, and the identification of etiological and diagnostic correlates of health, illness, and related dysfunction." In short, health psychology is concerned with improving the health of persons through the application of the principles and procedures of behavioral science, learning, and behavioral analysis/management.

The Spiritual-Health Connection:
Fact or Fantasy?

The central focus of this chapter is on the relationship between spirituality and health psychology while posing the central question: Is a healthy body and mind the legacy of a spiritual life-style? (We are quick to note here that, in separating mind and body, we are not invoking the outmoded mind-body dualism that has been clearly put to rest with the scientific data on the inseparable, closely intertwined brain-emotion-cognition-physical function links.) Conversely, are behavioral, psychological and social practices that represent the opposite extreme of the spiritual continuum—counterspiritual practices, if you will—more highly associated with disease, disability, and lower quality of health and life?

Although the necessary empirical work will be required to substantiate the positive effects of this faith-oriented life, the data that will be reviewed have suggested that, in the long run, a spiritually healthy life-style should also be a more physically healthy one. Though spiritual beliefs are not necessarily prescriptions for health, are such spiritual practices as prayer, meditation on religious ideas, and reading of religious materials (e.g., Torah, Koran, Bible), as well as adherence to spiritual teachings, all important contributors to health, particularly as they translate to changes in the probability of negative and positive health behaviors?

These latter questions are posed primarily with regard to the generally avoidable diseases and disorders, so very common today, that are principally attributable to maladaptive life-styles. We are not insinuating that all physically disabled or unhealthy individuals are that way because of some spiritual deficiency. On the contrary, taking the historical examples of the Jewish and Christian religions, suffering is encountered along the way for testing and building faith, or "spiritual muscles" (though there is also suffering that has no human explanation). But such experiences of suffering are hopefully balanced by experiences of joy, peace, and love, which would be predicted to extend naturally from the spiritually healthy way of life. The problem of the meaning of suffering, "why 'bad' things happen to 'good' people" (see Kushner, 1983), is not the focus of the present chapter and, therefore, will not be dealt with here.

The most logical starting point in investigating an association between spiritual orientations and practices, and health, is in the area so common to and, indeed, so often plaguing us all—stress and stress management. The following section will, therefore, address the research tying the two areas together and the consequent implications the spiritual life-style may have for stress-related disorders.

Stress, Health, and Spirituality

Stress and Health

Currently, there is much concern regarding the relationships between life stressors and health. There are several recent reviews of the literature documenting the negative health effects of stressors (see Krantz, Grunberg, & Baum, 1985; Miller, 1983). Researchers interested in the relationships among *stressors, stress*, and *health effects*, however, have had difficulty reaching a consensus even regarding definitions of these terms. Generally, however, they agree that stress involves a person's response to an actual or perceived threat or demand. In the industrialized world, as a rule, most of the threats and stressors have to do with oftentimes ambiguous daily hassles, life events, and challenges that can be perceived, interpreted, and reacted to in a variety of ways. Thus previous training (conditioning, modeling), beliefs about the world, and social contexts have much to do with the stressfulness of one's world.

It is not our purpose here to review this controversy or the voluminous literature on stress, and the interested reader is referred to the review papers mentioned earlier. Despite much debate concerning the definitions of stress/stressors, however, there does appear to be an emerging body of data to support negative health effects of stress (Baum, Grunberg, & Singer, 1982). Examples of such negative effects include chronic blood pressure elevation, ulcers, colitis, headaches, back and other chronic pain, diabetic disregulation, coronary heart disease, alcoholism, smoking, coronary sudden death, and immune system dysfunctions, possibly including cancer and other viruses, as well as even the common cold. Further, active clinicians can attest that one of the most common maladies confronting adults in the industrialized societies is that of chronic stress and stress-related disorders, from cardiovascular disease all the way down to stress-induced muscle tension and its related problems. For instance, chronic musculoskeletal tension may be viewed as a by-product of an inefficient, even maladaptive, coping system. Ultimately, it might be argued that the maladaptive coping strategies employed in these highly stressful times are often the antithesis of a spiritual life-style.

Perhaps most important, the *perception* of threat, or demand, more than anything else defines the individual's response to it and hence the level of stress experienced. These perceptions and especially the interpretations applied by the individual to the threat or demand control much, if not most, of the variance with regard to the pattern, duration, and possibly even the resulting harmfulness of the stress response (Bandura, 1986; Friedman & Rosenman, 1974; Glass, 1977; Meichenbaum & Jaremko, 1983; Scherwitz & Canick, 1987). The coloring of these perceptions and interpretations may, in turn, be significantly influenced by the individual's spiritual orientation or worldview. The following section will attempt to explore this potentially critical connection.

Stress and Spirituality

Viewing stress and coping from a spiritual angle, we find some interesting meta-associations within the stress research literature. For example, there is reason to believe that the spiritually oriented individual may be especially likely to perceive the stress-inducing demands, expectations, and potential threats of the world (including those that are internalized) as less upsetting and stressful; and those with more spiritually oriented life-styles may, in turn, experience fewer of the health consequences of stress than their lesser spiritually minded counterparts. Consider the following scenario:

Frank and Mike are both subjected to intense pressure from their boss to meet a nearly impossible deadline on a project. Frank believes in God, generally spends considerable time in prayer, spiritual meditation, and loving fellowship with others; is focused on people and relationships; tends to prefer working cooperatively rather than competitively; and has even been criticized by his wife for not being more materially oriented; when things "go wrong" for Frank, when he is provoked or if stressful events occur that may not be controllable, he tends to react by accepting the difficulty, lovingly asking for help or sharing with others, and surrendering control of the situation and any negative emotions to God through prayer, and so on. Mike, in contrast, does not believe in any power higher than himself, is relatively focused on personal achievement and material possessions (e.g., money accumulation), and he does not pray or meditate (though he exercises regularly and takes generally good care of himself physically); he feels that he must always be in control of himself and nearly every situation, and tends to struggle frequently with his own perfectionism; he believes only in himself and in the competitive marketplace—that he must strive against others to "rise to the top" and achieve all of which he is capable.

It may be a safe bet to assume that these two very different individuals would perceive, approach, and tackle the posed challenge in very different ways, and that there might be notable health consequences attached to their respective styles of dealing with this stress. While seemingly an extreme and very hypothetical illustration, we believe there may be more than a little truth to these life-style characterizations, and, furthermore, that their spiritual orientations as much as anything else will account for their relative effectiveness or ineffectiveness in processing and coping with the stress without negative health consequences. Nevertheless, this hypothetical scenario depicting contrasting stress coping styles of more versus less spiritual individuals (and the resulting health effects) is certainly one that is open to, and in need of, experimental verification or refutation.[1]

The degree of stress, and associated health decrement, experienced by an individual has been further related to the level of perceived commitment, control, and challenge in that person's life (Kobasa, 1979; Kobasa, Maddi, & Kahn, 1982). Consistent with an emerging concern within the field of stress research that there are no simple cause-effect relationships between stress and disease (Gentry & Kobasa, 1984), susceptibility to disease appears to result from some combination of susceptibility factors and resistance factors within the individual (Chesney & Gentry, 1982). For example, Kobasa and her colleagues were interested in the personal factors that mitigate the effects of stress. They found that, when persons develop strong commitments to their work and its meaningfulness, perceive the tasks that they perform as challenging rather than threatening, and operate with a sense of personal control over their environment, they are less likely to report negative stress or symptoms associated with serious illness. These data suggest the importance of internal factors in mitigating the health effects of external stressors. Moreover, these factors are dimensions relevant to the practice of spirituality.

It may be that, for a variety of stress-related problems, the more spiritual (see definition) the individual, the more likely he or she will be to "surrender" control (e.g., to a higher power) rather than anxiously fight against the "threat"; to employ "releasing" strategies such as prayer and meditation; and/or to seek out loving fellowship with other spiritually minded persons. This may result, in turn, in significantly fewer stress-related symptoms and disorders, and improved health and well-being, or at least no artificial reduction in days of life due to the ravages of stress and maladaptive coping.[2]

This all is not to say that the spiritually committed do not or will not suffer many of the same stress-mediated maladies and unhealthy habits as the less spiritual, or that spiritually focused thoughts, behaviors, and therapeutic goals will eliminate health risks. But, in general, one may argue that, if individuals are indeed adhering to spiritual dictates, they should be engaging in fewer health risk behaviors (e.g., disobedience to natural and societal laws; pre- or extramarital sex; addictive overconsumption of harmful substances) and they ought to, in turn, possess lower health risk, and greater happiness and overall quality of life, all other things being equal (James, 1903; McMillen, 1963; let us be careful here, to acknowledge that *some* religious practices may not be the healthiest things to do, e.g., the Pentecostals' poisonous snake handling!—though some, including ourselves, would be less prone to identify snake handling per se as a true or classical spiritual practice, at least not according to our definition, above).

Stress, Health, and Spiritual Worldview

Recall from our introductory remarks that spirituality among persons is characterized by strong commitment to a religious or spiritual worldview focusing on a developing relationship with God or some nonmaterial higher power, supreme being, or ultimate reality. For the spiritual person, this worldview further expands with time and serves as a central focus for making decisions and interpreting events. If, as Kobasa suggests, persons are able to withstand the effects of life stressors better when they find themselves committed to goals, even in the presence of such stressors, then we could expect that persons with a strong commitment to spirituality would be more resistant to the negative health effects of life stress. There is preliminary evidence to suggest that this is in fact the case. O'Brien (1982), for example, found that a positive religious perspective helped patients adapt to the stressors of hemodialysis; while Antonovsky (1979) found that holocaust victims who had a sense of the meaningfulness and purpose of life (e.g., God loved them and would care for them despite the man-made horror of the camps) not only survived, apparently unscathed in any significant way, but almost seemed to emerge stronger, as opposed to permanently scarred as so many others were because of the trauma.

Related to the concept of shared spiritual worldview, social support also appears to be an important factor mitigating the negative health effects of stress and trauma (Berkman & Breslow, 1983; Berkman & Syme, 1979; Cohen & Syme, 1985). Although it is not clear how social support functions, or the conditions under which it is more or less effective, the presence of social support appears to have positive health effects. Spirituality, with its emphasis on community, could thus be hypothesized to be associated with perceptions of increased social support during periods of stress. Finally, data obtained from the communities of Roseta (Bruhn, Chandler, Miller, Wolf, & Lynn, 1966; Wolf, 1976) and Alameda (Berkman & Breslow, 1983) are suggestive of the important roles that a sense of community and spirituality play in mitigating the effects of stress. This will be discussed in detail later in the chapter.

The Capturing of Spirituality: The Measurement Problem

If religious or spiritual beliefs are important to stress reduction and, in turn, health and well-being, then a critical issue that must be dealt with first is how one might objectively quantify spirituality. Without valid and reliable documentation of this spirituality dimension, it would be virtually impossible to determine any association with health and life quality. Thus before venturing any further into the research literature on the intriguing associations between stress, health and disease, and spirituality, it would be instructive to gain a better understanding of the methods and pitfalls of the quantification of spirituality and spiritual life-styles. A brief summary of the concepts, issues, and methods involved will now be presented, followed by an illustration from several relatively flawed, but nonetheless exciting, studies that have been conducted on prayer and health.

Global measurement of spirituality. A number of investigators have attempted to quantify dimensions of spirituality using a *global* approach to measurement. For example, one area of importance is that of the relationship between religious attitudes and religious behaviors. Fishbein and Ajzen (1974) have suggested that there is a strong relationship between religious attitudes and religious behaviors. They used comparisons among five methods for measuring religious attitudes and both single-item and multiple-item reports of religious behaviors. Although there is little relationship between single-item reports of religious behavior and measures of religious attitudes, there is a strong relationship between multiple-item scales of religious behavior and measures of religious attitude. Such findings lend support for the use of religious questionnaires for the empirical study of religious behavior.

The scientific measurement of spirituality per se has not been addressed specifically, but there are several questionnaire instruments available that focus on aspects relevant to our understanding of spirituality. We would like to note that Gorsuch (1984) has recently discussed the limitations of the questionnaire approach; however, at present, these are the only available instruments we are aware of for assessing religion and thus serve as the focus of our discussion.

While attempting to understand the nature of prejudice, Allport (1954) developed the intrinsic-extrinsic religious orientation scale (Allport & Ross, 1967). This instrument measures two motivational styles relevant to religious expression. The extrinsic style reflects religious expression for the sake of what can be gained for the individual by that expression or for living by religious mores. In contrast, the intrinsic dimension characterizes an approach centered on religion for the sake of religion. The intrinsic style represents a search for truth and desire to live out that truth regardless of the personal consequences.

Examination of the items on the Allport questionnaire indicates a blend of questions emphasizing both belief and practice. For the extrinsic scale, items include "The primary purpose of prayer is to gain relief and protection," "Although I am a religious person I refuse to let religious considerations influence my everyday affairs," and "What

religion offers me most is comfort when sorrows and misfortune strike."
Intrinsic scale items include "Quite often I have been keenly aware of the
presence of god or the Divine Being," "My religious beliefs are what
really lie behind my whole approach to life," and "It is important to me
to spend periods of time in private religious thought and meditation."
The items in the extrinsic-intrinsic scale capture some of the dimensions
of spirituality but leave other dimensions such as practice of prayer or
active fellowship with others relatively untapped. As an empirical scale,
however, the extrinsic-intrinsic religious orientation appears to represent
a valid and reliable instrument for understanding several dimensions of
religious experience (Robinson & Shaver, 1973).

Glock and Stark (1965) developed a scale of religious commitment
based upon an extensive theoretical analysis of the means by which an
individual could be considered "religious." Items in this scale were
developed from the identification of five dimensions of religious
experience. These dimensions included (a) experiential, which involves
experiences with God; (b) ideological, or core beliefs about God; (c)
ritualistic, including activities such as prayer and meditation; (d)
intellectual, representing beliefs about the faith; and (e) consequential,
or the effects the beliefs have on the individual's life. Although data
relating reliability and validity for these scales are not conclusive or
obtained from broad samples, Faulkner and DeJong (1966) reported
reliabilities ranging from .90 to .94 for their version of an instrument
measuring the five dimensions developed by Glock and Stark.

Other scales, such as that for mysticism (Hood, 1975) and religiosity
(King & Hunt, 1975) are also used for the evaluation of religious
dimensions (see Pattison, Chapter 9, Table 9.2). In fact, Gorsuch (1984,
p. 234) has stated that "scales are available in sufficient variety for most
any task in the psychology of religion." Therefore, it appears that there
are a variety of existing measures available to assist in the empirical
study of the relationships between health psychology and spirituality.
Before this topic is concluded, however, the question of the correspondence between questionnaires on religious attitudes or beliefs and
actual behavior must be considered.

Multimodal spirituality assessment. Indeed, when attempting to
quantify something as elusive and complex as spirituality, one must be
sure to employ a measure that truly reflects these core beliefs. Yet, to
calibrate reliably the overall effect of spirituality on health requires
more than merely using a questionnaire with reasonable face and/or
construct validity.

Approximately 20 years ago, the field of clinical psychology was called to a newer age of scientific credibility through the use of multiple modality measurement of behavior (Lang, 1971). Since that time, behavioral scientists have generally tried to include measures from the two objective measurement modalities of observed motor and physiological responses, to go along with the subjective modality of self-reported thoughts, perceptions, emotions, and beliefs. Thus, while individuals may report that they are quite peaceful and relaxed, their heart rate and muscle tension might be extremely high, and they may continue to avoid certain people or situations that do not, in fact, pose any threat. Much research has indicated that these three modalities are frequently independent of one another (as we now know that thoughts, perceptions, emotions, and beliefs might also be independently experienced and expressed) and must, therefore, be assessed separately before conclusions might be made as to the overall response of the individual. Much more recently, this trend toward multiple modality measurement has begun to invade research on the psychology of religion and spirituality, bringing with it the welcome potential for greater scientific credibility.

Unfortunately, the process of developing, refining, and/or adapting the measurement instruments and procedures to quantify spirituality has only just begun, as this current volume no doubt will suggest to the reader. As in many fields of scientific endeavor, the study of spiritual influences on health and life quality will be limited in direct proportion to the capacity of the current measurement technologies to capture precisely, and to quantify objectively and reliably, the construct. The studies to date have employed relatively crude cognitive, attitude, and belief self-report measures, while only relatively recently have physiological and behavioral measures been added (see the following illustrations). The studies on spirituality and health will continue to be at least somewhat scientifically suspect until we achieve a more precise isolation and quantification of the measurable dimensions of spirituality—particularly in conjunction with well-measured and normed response systems (i.e., cognitive, emotional, physiological, behavioral). We recognize that this credibility gap is being closed, due in part to multiple-response tracking and the increasing use of more reliable indices of at least outward spirituality (e.g., church/synagogue attendance, experimental replication of spiritual practices under controlled circumstances), as will be illustrated in the remaining portions of the chapter.

The following section provides what we believe to be an interesting analogue illustrating this needed progression in the quality and scope of studies in this area, as well as the special importance of multiple modality measurement to this type of inquiry.

Stress, Prayer, and Health

Some study has been devoted to determining whether prayer, a common manifestation of spirituality, can serve to reduce stress and treat illness. Although prayer is one of the oldest forms of therapeutic intervention, and continues to be commonly conducted by physicians (a recent survey conducted by *MD Magazine* indicated that two-thirds of a sample of 126 physicians reported they had prayed for their patients), it has received relatively little attention in the scientific literature. Three studies are of particular interest in the present context.

In the first formal study on the psychological and psychophysiological healing effects of prayer that we know of, Parker and St. Johns (1957) assigned 45 male and female volunteer psychotherapy clients to nine months of either weekly individual (psycho)therapy, daily individual (home) prayer, or weekly structured group prayer (daily, individual practice). Many of the "volunteers," referred from physicians, clergy, and so on, had symptoms of stress such as anxiety, depression, headache, back pain, "nervous breakdown," hostility, and nervous tics. Regrettably, the investigators failed to assign subjects randomly to treatment groups, they did not objectively document symptomatology, and, even more unfortunately, the only pre- and posttesting done was traditional (psychodynamic) tests such as the Rorschach Ink Blot Test, TAT, and word association tests. According to the investigators, at the end of the nine-month period, self-report data and psychological testing (conducted by an "impartial tester") indicated that those in the structured prayer therapy group showed the most improvement (72% reported improvement), as compared to 65% showing improvement in the psychotherapy group, while none of the 15 subjects in the random (home prayer) group improved. No tests of statistical significance were conducted to determine if differences reliably distinguished between the groups; and the fact that subjects were selectively assigned to particular treatment groups renders the results scientifically questionable. Nevertheless, the investigators stated that only in the structured group prayer therapy subjects was there any evidence of "complete healing" of symptoms, confirming their hypothesis that this would be the superior group.

A better-controlled prayer-stress study was conducted by Carlson, Bacaseta, and Simanton (1986) in which multimodal measurement was employed. Volunteer (nonclinical) students from a large Christian college in the Midwest were randomly assigned to one of the following: prayer and scriptural/spiritual meditation, progressive muscle relaxation training, or wait-list control. Self-report, questionnaire, personality, and standard psychophysiological (heart rate, EMG, and finger temperature) measures of state and trait anxiety, depression, and arousal were obtained before and following three weeks of three-times-per-week laboratory sessions. There were no pretreatment differences on any of these measures across groups. At the conclusion of the experiment, the prayer and devotional meditation group was found to exhibit significantly lower anger and anxiety than the other two groups, but there were no differences in the three groups with respect to physiological indices of stress. Unfortunately, due to the very brief (three-week) duration of the study, it was not possible to determine any differential long-term effects on either the self-report or the physiological measures of stress. Although the groups were found to be equivalent on a self-report measure of spirituality (Allport & Ross, 1967), the use of an analogue population of students who were religiously committed may have biased the results in favor of the prayer and devotional meditation group.

A third, even more highly controlled prayer study conducted by Byrd (1984) has perhaps the most exciting implications. Over a 10-month period, 393 patients admitted to a hospital coronary care unit in acute distress (i.e., for heart attack) were randomly assigned to either an intercessory prayer group (IP) or a no prayer group (NP) control condition. A group of Christians prayed for the individuals in the IP group outside the hospital, while the NP group received no prayer. Patients and hospital personnel were all blind to group assignment. At the conclusion of the study, patients in the IP group as compared to the NP group were found to have significantly less pulmonary edema ($p <$ 0.03), were intubated less frequently ($p < 0.002$), and required fewer antibiotics ($p < 0.007$). Unfortunately, no data were presented to indicate whether other medical or health indices were obtained, or how they compared across the two groups.

Despite these somewhat dramatic findings, the studies on prayer suffer from a number of inherent methodological problems that limit their reliability and generalizability and, consequently, their usefulness to the scientific body. First, the use of only spiritually oriented, highly select subjects in the former two studies may well have biased the results in the predicted direction (i.e., toward demonstrating the superiority of systematic prayer as opposed to the secular interventions). A more representative and better-controlled test would be to balance the spiritual/secular orientations of the subjects with the two treatment orientations in a 2×2 randomized design. In this way, each treatment orientation could be tested on subjects with both concordant and discordant orientations. Other limitations include inadequate quality, scope, and duration of (collateral) health measures; insufficient follow-up; nonblinded experiments and data collectors; inappropriate or no statistical analysis; and/or weak documentation of quality and quantity of treatment. Because of these drawbacks, no conclusions can be drawn at this time, although there would appear to be excellent cause to investigate these intriguing associations in a more comprehensive scientific manner.

Relaxation, Meditation, Prayer:
A *Peace* Continuum?

One of the chief endpoints targeted by the practices of many spiritual systems is the experience of inner *peace*, in its deepest and most profound sense.[3] Throughout the centuries, much has been written about achieving this state of mind, or spirit (e.g., Foster, 1978). While many have argued as to the best way to approach this goal, few have disputed its desirability. A very recent addition to this historical pursuit of peace and serenity would have to be the field of behavioral medicine/health psychology. In fact, over the past twenty years or so, secular scientific attempts to teach inner peace have stemmed in large part from Jacobson's pioneering work on progressive relaxation (Jacobson, 1939); subsequently included were a number of secular relaxation and meditation techniques for treating a variety of stress-related disorders (e.g., hypertension, Raynauds syndrome, dysmenor-rhea, headache, Type A Coronary Prone Behavior Pattern) as well as for producing profound calm and states of well-being in higher stress nonclinical populations.

Some of the earliest studies on the effects of relaxation on health and bioregulation employed secular meditation, relaxation, and/or biofeed-back, in an effort to reproduce the level of biological self-control observed in Eastern spiritual meditators (see Wallace & Benson, 1972).

These relaxation/peace-induction interventions soon incorporated a number of the spiritual techniques. For example, the resulting combinations of relaxation/spiritual meditation techniques included various forms of spiritually oriented meditations such as TM (Transcendental Meditation) and Zen (Wallace & Benson, 1972), as well as yogic meditation and exercises (Datey, Deshmukh, Dalvi, & Vinekar, 1969; Patel, 1975). They may have stopped short in this integration, however. Is it possible that the secular meditation and relaxation techniques currently in use in the field of behavioral medicine/health psychology, as powerful as they may be in producing relaxation and mental calm, and in reversing certain maladaptive physical conditions (including enhancement of immune function; Kiecolt-Glaser & Glaser, 1987), may be yet approximations of the profound biological and psychological *peace* achievable through deep spiritual meditation and prayer (see Foster, 1978), especially when practiced by those who value a spiritual orientation? This is an answerable question for which few studies have been addressed.

At its most effective, relaxation would appear to share common ground with spiritual meditation/prayer in that they both tend to require (a) a trusting, passive attitude of release and surrender of control (much like that required for effective hypnosis); (b) separation from distracting environmental events and noise (in the very experienced, prayer and meditation, and possibly relaxation, may be achievable without seclusion, though probably not during the early learning stages); (c) active focusing upon or repetition of a mental strategy (as opposed to sleeping); (d) task awareness; and (e) deep muscle relaxation (see Jacob, Kraemer, & Agras, 1977). It may also be that a deep abiding belief in both the meaning and the efficacy of the procedure, such as might be expected in devout prayers, will significantly enhance the effect or perhaps even open the gates to a much more profound peace and healthful effect. We believe the studies reviewed in this chapter may be viewed as at least partially supportive of this hypothesis, or at least enough to warrant additional careful investigation. At the very least, in a clinical setting with spiritually committed clients, therapists might enhance healing and induce peace and stress reduction most efficiently through primary or adjunctive use of meditation and prayer, whereas, in lesser spiritual clients, progressive relaxation may have advantages (though the relative efficacy of these approaches may well be differential).

Clearly, more research is needed, especially with precise, comprehensive measurement of health change and spiritual practices and beliefs, to ascertain if prayer and spiritual meditation truly bring more profound peace or deep relaxation (and hence greater health and freedom from stress-related disease). If nothing more, spiritually driven faith and belief may nevertheless enhance compliance to the relaxation/stress management treatment (DiMatteo & DiNicola, 1982; Haynes, Taylor, & Sackett, 1979), though they may in and of themselves add to the overall effectiveness of the health intervention (Epstein, 1984). At least for the religiously or spiritually committed, this raises the question of whether there can be a more significant inroad or starting point to this type of health-enhancing expectancy than through the spiritual/religious network of the individual. This is a fascinating empirical question that can, and should, in our opinion, be carefully tested.

We hope that these studies will be forthcoming, and that the best techniques of psychological science will be employed. For example, we feel strongly that, to be a fair test, seasoned prayers with strong beliefs in God or in their higher power should be employed in all studies of the healing effects of prayer and other spiritual methods, such as was attempted in the Byrd (1984) study, to ensure the representativeness of the intervention as well as the scientific validity of the test. Further, we would hasten to add that in no way do we believe that positive or negative results would necessarily prove or disprove the tenets of the particular faith. On the contrary, we believe that more and better science should be brought into the realm of spiritual and religious practice to indicate where spiritual beliefs and practices may be helpful and healthful to both the person and community, as well as where more effective avenues and alternatives—within the context of their belief systems—might be considered and tested. At this point, it will be useful to look at the relationship of other, more specific spiritual teachings and practices to health and disease.

Health, Disease, and Spiritual Living

The biblical quote opening this chapter suggests that engaging in certain prescribed spiritual and religious practices, and avoiding alternative (high-risk) behaviors, will result in less suffering and ill health in followers. It is indeed noteworthy that, at the time this and other biblical prescriptions and proscriptions were recorded, over 3000 years ago, many of the major diseases were infectious in nature, and, more important, there would be no body of knowledge or science of medicine and disease to alert them to these health problems for another 2900+ years! Many of the these debilitating—and life-threatening maladies, we now know, were due to a lack of personal and societal cleanliness, that is, sewage contamination in water and food supplies; disease-carrying rodents and other "unclean" animals; poor food selection, preparation, and eating practices; sexually transmitted diseases; and human passing of germs—things, as shall be seen, the Torah and Bible had much to say about.

Even today, while many of those diseases have been nearly eradicated through better sanitation and other public health practices such as immunizations, other almost equally lethal diseases of life-style have taken their place. These more "modern" diseases are frequently disorders that stem from living in the "fast lane" of high stress, addictive overconsumption, fast foods, energy-saving devices, and sexual "liberation." Further, recent consolidations and meta-analyses of the evidence on the psychosocial correlates of disease (including the so-called psychosomatic illnesses) suggest the existence of a generic disease-prone personality, related most strongly to asthma, arthritis, ulcers, headaches, and especially coronary heart disease (Booth-Kewley & Friedman, 1987; Friedman & Booth-Kewley, 1987). These personality-grounded disease risk factors primarily include depression, anger/hostility, and anxiety (Scherwitz & Canick, 1987), and may be seen as the inevitable psychological and emotional consequences (at least in part) of habitual violation of important spiritual "laws" and practices that have been handed down from generation to generation (whether divinely inspired or not; Bergin, 1980; McMillen, 1963).

These disorders of life-style and the apparent link with spiritual practices (or, in this case, failure to adhere to spiritual practices) will be discussed in greater detail in the following sections of this chapter. At this point, it would be useful and perhaps even enlightening to note some examples of spiritual wisdom and faith-governed (some might say "blind" faith-governed) health practices that emanate from the spiritual system we are most familiar with—the Judeo-Christian heritage.

Spiritual Doctrine:
Inspired Health Wisdom?

In the Jewish Torah, there appears a listing of proscriptions and prescriptions for the conducting of almost every imaginable situation, circumstance, or interaction, including legal, business, and social situations, the care and keeping of the body, and even rules governing physical contact between individuals. Many of these rules and commandments ultimately concerned or affected the health of the individual and the community. Although the health rationale was apparently not provided at the time, it was presented more as loyal obedience to God's laws. For example, it declared people "unclean" if they so much as touched a dead body or animal, or even the clothing of the deceased, commanding them to wash body and clothing and be removed from others for seven days. Interestingly, this was long before the role of germs was known in the cause and spread of disease. In terms of our present knowledge of health and disease processes, those tribes and communities who obeyed this one command would presumably have been much more likely to live longer, more healthful lives, not to mention surviving as a culture (McMillen, 1963). In fact, it has been said that relatively fewer Jews died of the bubonic plague that nearly eradicated Europe because they adhered to their then ancient spiritual practice of washing their hands (Mendelsohn, 1987). Another fascinating spiritual practice that may have important public health implications was the early Jewish practice of nursing their children to two years of age (see Abraham and Sarah's son Isaac, Genesis 21:8). This may have helped to control overpopulation, and the problems that went with it such as starvation during years of famine, by retarding ovulation and conception during the two years following birth—resulting in a minimum of nearly four years between conception and the birth of a new child (Mendelsohn, 1987).

A further example of spiritually influenced health practices is the spiritual prescription of circumcision on the eighth day after birth. This seemingly barbaric practice had two profound health rationales unbeknownst to the Tribes of Israel. Though not nearly the health problem today as then, penile cancer in men was an important cause of death, and at least partially attributable to the male's foreskin trapping bacteria-laden secretions and debris (and the failure to wash conscientiously in that area). In addition, recent data suggest that uncircumsized men may be more vulnerable to sexually transmitted diseases such as herpes and AIDS. Thus this became not only a sign to the world of God's covenant with the "chosen ones," but also a very wise preventive health measure at that time. Further, it was vital that this be done on the eighth day of life, given that the blood clotting factor, insufficient before then, peaks on the eighth day—consequently, the safest day to perform that type of surgery (McMillen, 1963). The command also included using a newly cut flint stone that was sharper and freer of germs than other cutting instruments in common use then.

An additional health practice included the prescriptions and proscriptions of sexual contact, helping further to minimize sexually transmitted diseases that were an even more significant public health problem then as now (particularly because there was no effective, if not life-saving, treatment until this century). These proscriptions against premarital sex and multiple sex partners are still relevant today, in our age of frightening explosions in the sexually transmitted devastators of quality and quantity of life—respectively, herpes and AIDS—as well as other multiple-partner-related diseases such as cervical cancer (McMillen, 1963). Finally, the historical proscriptions against drunkenness and other "excesses of the flesh" (gluttony; Type A pursuit of money and power) and emotions (e.g., bitterness and guile) and the corresponding call for moderation in all things have clear health implications even today.

Spirituality and Disorders of Life-Style

A number of diseases have been related to behavioral, psychological, and social dysfunction, oftentimes referred to as unhealthy life-styles (some have even called this the American Lifestyle; Farquhar, 1979). Probably the best example of these disorders are the cardiovascular diseases, principally coronary heart disease (CHD). Behavioral, psychological, and social factors that are associated with the development, progression, and ultimate lethality of heart and other diseases include the addictive overconsumption of animal fat (hypercholesterolemia, hypertension, obesity), salt, and foods rich in calories (hypertension, obesity, diabetes); tobacco (oral, lung, and other cancers, and pulmonary disease, as well as CHD, and peripheral vascular disease); and alcohol (liver, gastrointestinal, heart, and brain disease; accidents) (Levy & Moskowitz, 1982; Pooling Project Research Group, 1975). The highly stressful and hostile Type A Coronary Prone Behavior Pattern has also been correlated with CHD morbidity and mortality (Review Panel on Coronary-Prone Behavior and Coronary Heart Disease, 1981). More recently, high stress patterns of relating to one's environment and others have been traced to child-rearing practices (Thoresen, 1987) and have been connected with disorders of the immune system as well as the cardiovascular system. For example, those who divorce often experience significant detrimental changes in their immune function as well as significant psychological trauma and life disruption (Kiecolt-Glaser, 1986).

There is an important question here: Do these diseases of life-style and health regulation occur in part because of our individual or collective failure to adhere to spiritual principles and practices? Or, a question that might be easier to answer: Do people who believe in God; engage in worship, prayer, and fellowship with other believers; *and/or* who make bona fide attempts to bring their own behavior and thoughts into correspondence with these spiritual teachings have better health through more effective avoidance of the unhealthy patterns that give rise to the disease processes? While there are few hard data on this, it is instructive to view the spiritual practices and beliefs as they relate to some of these disease categories.

Overconsumption Versus a Spiritual Life

Many religious and spiritual doctrines include as a basic tenet that adherents should regularly engage in the practice of abstinence or at least regular fasting from harmful or potentially harmful substances such as (certain) foods, alcohol, and tobacco. These practices may be spiritually inspired (e.g., to sacrifice for God and/or to break the hold the "flesh" has on the spirit), may be to cleanse the body periodically from the health risks of overconsumption (e.g., toxin buildup), and may have important health benefits. For example, Panush (1987) has provided evidence supporting the value of fasting in the reduction of pain and inflammation in rheumatic disease, whereas the most recent data on heart disease and diet indicates that vegetarian fasting, as practiced by some spiritual sects, and low fat/low cholesterol diets may help prevent coronary heart disease (Lipid Research Clinics Program, 1984a, 1984b). Many religions have traditionally banned certain substances that our scientific technology has only recently found to be harmful, such as tobacco and alcohol, or that at one time were unhealthful, such as eating pork and other "unclean" meats (e.g., uncooked, blood-infected meats).

Clearly, the extreme health risks of tobacco and excess dietary fat and alcohol have been very well established. Spiritually oriented abstinence programs of certain religions and self-help organizations, such as Alcoholics Anonymous, Smokers Anonymous, and Overeaters Anonymous, have been particularly popular as well as useful—especially for those who are more spiritually oriented and who have had problems in the past with controlling their appetitive desires. In light of the extreme difficulty of changing addictive or compulsive behaviors with even modern behavioral and cognitive interventions, we in the behavioral and social sciences are becoming increasingly aware of the potency and resistance to extinction of rule-governed behavior, as illustrated by spiritual belief systems and faiths, and the possibility of harnessing this power in this therapeutic context. For example, therapists treating compulsive overeaters or drinkers or smokers may do well to incorporate both their rationale and their approach to therapy with the client's spiritual orientation, such as focusing on spiritual commands and methods for controlling or abstaining from behaviors or substances that may be harmful (e.g., smoking, alcohol, anger, worry). Use of the spiritual approaches of divine meditation and prayer, regular worship, learning to be unconditionally loving, and increasing spiritually oriented fellowship and social support may be for many a much more important starting point for and possibly more effective overall source of disease prevention and control than secular counseling, contingency management, or other therapies by themselves.

Spiritual Koinonia and Health

As in the area of stress management noted previously, the role of family and community support in the maintenance of physical health has also received much recent attention. Strong social support correlates highly not only with superior health (Sarason, Sarason, Potter, & Antoni, 1985), but also with adherence to health programs (Martin & Dubbert, 1982, 1985). One of the key characteristics of many religious systems is regular (if not daily) fellowship with other believers. The spiritual fellowship/support provided by others may relate to improved quality and perhaps quantity of life. Loneliness, withdrawal, depression, and death of a loved-one (especially when there is no loving community to surround and support the survivor) can often have profound effects on the health and well-being of an individual.[4] Given the importance of cognitive processing and beliefs to coping with stress (Bandura, 1986), it would make sense then that an individual's ultimate beliefs and interpretations with regard to suffering and life are critical to how they bounce back from life's difficulties. Further, having a loving, highly supportive community of like-believers would also seem an extremely valuable, if not essential, ingredient to a healthy and happy life. Indeed, there is even some emerging evidence that the positive type of spiritual fellowship we are referring to may add significantly to the overall health and life-quality enhancement that may be attributed to social support without the spiritual connection.

The Roseta community study (Bruhn et al., 1966; Wolf, 1976) is pertinent here. In this Italian American community located in eastern Pennsylvania, it was found that the community's low incidence of deaths due to heart disease was associated with a strong sense of community where almost all members of the group supported one another, had strong religious beliefs and regular participation in religious activities, and clear role expectations for members of the community. Interestingly, as the community became more enmeshed in the prevailing American culture during the 1960s and 1970s, deaths from heart disease began to increase markedly (Bruhn & Wolf, 1978). Although the results are not conclusive, particularly because we know that acculturation can also result in dietary and other changes in lifestyle that may not have spiritual significance, they do provide initial encouragement for further explorations of the relationships between spirituality and coping with life stressors.

The potentially confounding effects of changes in diet and other nonspiritually legislated health changes were controlled for in a large study conducted in Alameda, California. The Alameda County Study (Berkman & Breslow, 1983) provides additional intriguing associations between spiritually oriented social support and health and disease. In this large epidemiologic study (6928 people were studied over a 20-year period), those who reported membership in a church were found to have significantly lower mortality than those who reported no church membership, and this relationship appeared to be independent of health behaviors per se (e.g., smoking, diet). For example, in the 30-49 age group, church member mortality was 1.4% while mortality for non-church members was over twice as much (3.9%, $p < .05$). Further, for this same age group, mortality rates for church members was lower than that for people with other important social support such as having high contact with friends and relatives (1.9%) and other (nonspiritual) group membership (2.4%).

Regularity of worship appears to be linked with this community health effect, particularly with respect to quality of life—a factor growing in importance to overall health and vital in its own right, as noted in the current epidemiological/health research. Meadow (1984) has summarized the studies correlating level of faith in God, and, more so, regularity of church attendance, and measures of well-being and life satisfactions. In one study, life satisfaction was best predicted by frequency of church attendance, whereas marital and family satisfaction and general positive feeling states were predicted best by satisfaction from religion (Hadaway & Roof, 1978; McNamara & St. George, 1979). Other epidemiologic studies have noted that, as compared to non-frequent churchgoers, frequent churchgoers have a lower risk of heart disease, pulmonary emphysema, suicide, cirrhosis of the liver, high blood pressure, and tuberculosis (Comstock, Abbey, & Lundin, 1970; Comstock & Partridge, 1972; Graham et al., 1978). Finally, an Israeli study found a lower incidence of myocardial infarction among more religious Jews (Medalie, Kahn, Neufeld, Riss, & Goldbourt, 1973).

More research in this area would be useful to document better the importance of social support or, more specifically, fellowship. It may be that in the final analysis, God-worshiping and/or loving spiritual fellowship will be shown to be superior to more secular social support. We believe this would be a fruitful area of inquiry, and are anxious to see more research exploring these issues.

Coronary Heart Disease and Spirituality

Broadly, several studies discussed previously have noted a negative association between church attendance (at least a surface measure of spirituality) and specific incidence of cardiovascular morbidity and mortality (Kaplan, 1976), although other investigators have found this evidence to be mixed at best (e.g., Jenkins, 1971). Kaplan has reported that, in a five-year ischemic incidence study conducted in Israel, Medalie indicated that age-adjusted CHD rates per thousand were 29 for orthodox Jews, 37 for traditional Jews, and 56 for nonreligious Jews. Unfortunately, diet or other risk factors were not taken into consideration in this study. A North Carolina study (Graham et al., 1978) also found that blood pressure levels were consistently lower in frequent as opposed to infrequent churchgoers. This difference was not due to differences in age, obesity, smoking, or socioeconomic status. Also familiar to the reader will probably be the epidemiologic data indicating lower health risks in religious populations such as the Mormons and the Amish. One must consider instrumental in this spirituality-health connection the spiritual practices of prayer, loving fellowship, and worship, along with the more commonly cited and worldly practices of abstaining from tobacco and alcohol, as well as their practice of avoiding work stress through choosing vocations and communities that do not reinforce workaholism.

Stress, Type A coronary-prone behavior, and spirituality. Type A Coronary Prone Behavior Pattern, while at times too loosely defined to satisfy the laboratory scientist, is a broad label used to describe a syndrome characterizing individuals who more frequently than non-Type As (Type B, they are termed by some) develop and/or die from coronary heart disease, our nation's number one killer (Review Panel on Coronary-Prone Behavior and Coronary Heart Disease, 1981; Rosenman et al., 1984). In fact, 51% of all deaths today are attributable to cardiovascular disease (Levy & Moskowitz, 1982), with the majority of those being due to CHD. It is also important to note that a significant number of coronary patients are found to have Type A Behavior Pattern (Blumenthal, Williams, & Kong, 1978), which has independently been related to increased morbidity and mortality over and above that which is attributed to other risk factors (Review Panel on CPBP and CHD, 1981; Rosenman et al., 1984).

Type A behavior has been called by some the "hurry sickness," and is characterized by a highly competitive, extremely impatient, hostile individual attempting rigidly to control an oftentimes out-of-control world (Friedman & Rosenman, 1974; Powell & Thoresen, 1987; Thoresen, 1987). Paradoxically, Type As expend tremendous emotional, physical, and even spiritual energy and resources on ill-fated efforts to control themselves and others *perfectly* (Glass, 1977). Some have described the behavioral and psychological *modus operandi* of these "world policemen" (most Type As are male, not surprisingly), as suggesting that the individual would "rather die than fail"; that their actions and (over)reactions reflect the deeply ingrained belief that they exist in an unforgiving world of diminishing resources, filled with other equally hostile, untrustworthy people, all competing for the same limited supply of goods, achievements, pleasures, and social approval (Friedman, 1978; Friedman & Rosenman, 1974; Powell & Thoresen, 1987).

In many ways, the Type A represents the opposite end of the spiritual continuum that we defined earlier. That is, in a very real sense they seem to be "playing God," attempting to be perfect, but in a very un-God-like fashion—impatiently, unforgivingly, and unlovingly forcing everyone, including themselves, to conform to their definition of perfection, usually for self-serving reasons. They seem to be faith*less*ly fighting, alone, for survival in an untrustworthy and hostile environment—a task representing the most elementary level of existence according to Maslow's (1970) basic needs hierarchy. Clearly, in such a hostile and seemingly meaningless world, spiritual growth and unselfish love are likely the last things on the mind and in the behavior of the Type A individual. A profound personal insecurity tells them they have little worth other than what they can accomplish or achieve, and thus the amount of momentary social approval they can obtain becomes their only barometer of worthwhileness and success (Friedman, 1978; Friedman & Rosenman, 1974; Powell & Thoresen, 1987).

This maladaptive pattern appears to extend back into childhood (Thoresen, 1987), and may be passed on through punitive overemphasis of material acquisition and competitive achievement, and strict conditional loving and modeling geared to this end (Glass, 1977; Thoresen, 1987). Through these mechanisms, this destructive pattern of relating to oneself, others, and the world would likely be passed on—barring some dramatic change in the person (e.g., religious/spiritual conversion, serious illness) or environment (moving family to Fiji)—from generation to generation (i.e., "the sins of the father will be visited upon the children"). This scenario stands in sharp contrast to the spiritually fulfilled individual who is more likely to receive self-worth and happiness through who he or she is, rather than what he or she does, seeking peace, humility, acceptance, love, forgiveness, guidance, meaning, and purpose in life, as well as strength, through contact (prayer, meditation, worship) with God or a higher power, adherence to unchanging spiritual dictates, and loving fellowship within their spiritual community.

Looking more closely at this complex pattern of profoundly maladaptive behavior, we find that the most recent data single out three virulent core patterns that are most associated with the coronary disease process itself: (a) hostility, cynicism, and/or suppressed anger (Chesney & Rosenman, 1985; Powell & Thoresen, 1987; Williams, 1984); (b) self-absorption or narcissism (Scherwitz, Berton, & Leventhal, 1978; Scherwitz, Granditz, Graham, Buehler, & Billings, 1986); and (c) depression (Booth-Kewley & Friedman, 1987; Powell & Thoresen, 1987; Thoresen, 1987). A related pattern consists of an emotional, physiological, and behavioral hyperreactivity to stress and perceived threat and challenge (see *Behavioral Medicine Update*, 1984, volume 6, issues 3 and 4, for a more thorough discussion of Type A Behavior Pattern with particular emphasis on these hyperreactivity patterns that characterize the coronary-prone individual).

Interestingly, when self-absorption (as reflected by increased use of the pronouns *I* and *my*, in particular) occurs in conjunction with hurried, pressing speech, the association with coronary heart disease is enhanced (Scherwitz & Canick, 1987). Increased self-preoccupation, as evidenced by the self-referencing in speech, has also been found to be even more predictive of history of previous heart attack, CHD severity, blood pressure elevation, number of occluded arteries, and CHD mortality than global Type A alone (Scherwitz & Canick, 1987; Scherwitz et al., 1978), whereas self-referencing has been found to be more common in depressed and anxious individuals (Scherwitz & Canick, 1987). Further, when extreme Type A coexists with high levels of self-referencing, they apparently interact to elevate further the coronary risk (Scherwitz & Canick, 1987). Similarly, Friedman et al. (1984) have observed that the more self-absorbed, egocentric Type As had the hardest time changing their Type A behavior pattern.

Scherwitz theorizes that it is the constant search for identity and self by a deeply insecure person that characterizes the Type A's struggle that often ends in the "relief" of a heart attack (Friedman & Ulmer, 1984; Scherwitz & Canick, 1987). One might easily argue that each of these behavior patterns and world perceptions comprises states of mind, body, and spirit that are just the opposite of that for which the major spiritual systems strive.

A particularly striking characteristic common to the Type A Behavior Pattern in general, and more specifically to the three lethal core components, is that these have been described as individuals who do not, and may not know how to, *love*. In fact, Friedman (1978) and Thoresen (1987; Powell & Thoresen, 1985, 1987; Powell et al., 1986) suggest that Type A Coronary Prone Behavior Pattern may be described as a sort of spiritual bankruptcy, linking (appropriately, we believe) love with spirituality. Conversely, they would further suggest (as we would) that the apparent absence of love in the case of Type A Behavior Pattern is related to nonspiritual (if not antispiritual) expectations, beliefs, and practices, such as materialism, perfectionism, and narcissism/self-absorption. Even more provocative than this notion is the fact that the approach taken by these clinical scientists to modify this lethal behavior pattern has strong spiritual overtones.

Modifying Type A: Teaching spirituality. An especially germane biblical exhortation, recorded over 1900 years ago, represents one of the earliest descriptions of, as well as calls toward, a Type B spiritual life-style:

> But the fruit of the spirit is love, joy, peace, patience, kindness, goodness, faithfulness, gentleness, and self-control. (Galatians 5:22; NIV)

Of no little significance, then, is the fact that the most effective "modern" treatment to modify (i.e., modulate) this Type A Pattern, developed and implemented by Thoresen, Powell and Friedman (1985), appears to have at its core an extensive (and similar) spiritual development component. Their treatment of these patients who have usually already experienced their first heart attack and/or coronary bypass operation includes thorough instruction in shaping and reinforcement in the ways of *loving* others (and themselves), and in *surrendering control* of the world—interestingly, two basic tenets of many religions.

At a recent workshop on modifying Type A Behavior (Powell et al., 1986), Powell clearly indicated that a most critical aspect of their program was to teach the Type As how to give and receive love on a daily basis—to view the world not as a hostile place that needs to be combated but as one that can be cooperative, loving, and peaceful, if not joyous (see Powell & Thoresen, 1987, for an excellent and detailed description of their treatment process). Interestingly, Thoresen (1987) has pointed out that, when the Type A patients were questioned as to what they thought was the most important component within the program, the majority replied that it was the hand-holding benediction—a spiritually "neutral" prayer finishing with "Amen" and extolling the importance of love and changing their ways together—that closed each therapy session.

Another spiritually grounded exercise employed by Thoresen and colleagues in altering the destructive Type A Behavior Pattern components focuses on hostile and self-centered impatience. The teaching of *humble patience*, a goal of many spiritual systems, is accomplished through repeated modeling, role-plays, group support, and prescribed in vivo trials (e.g., seeking out the longest and slowest-moving lines in supermarkets, suppressing emotional upset, and learning to tolerate easily, if not enjoy, the wait) until patients can successfully and consistently wait in lines without getting upset.[5]

To defuse further the ravages of the most destructive elements of the Type A Behavior Pattern, the patients were also shaped in the elementary behaviors of *love* and *acceptance*. For example, some patients had to be (re)trained in smiling at others (for many it had been a long time since they were able to smile spontaneously), while modeling, practice in therapy, and homework assignments (i.e., smile at a certain number of people per day) had to be required before this elementary loving behavior was relearned and generalized to their nontherapy environments (Powell et al., 1986). In a very real sense, patients also had to be taught to stop "playing God." They were subsequently coached in surrendering control of the world, others, and, even, to some extent, themselves, and to assume a posture of unperturbed acceptance of those many things (including their own personal limitations) that could not or should not be changed, or that could only be changed through the too-high cost of constant effort, worry, and poor health. The spiritual concept of grace (unmerited favor) was introduced in a more secular context but the message was basically the same: It is wise and very desirable to focus on, and be open to receive, the many wonderful things of life that do not have to be earned, but that are there for the asking or the receiving (e.g., love, friendship, serenity, rest, laughter, joy, fun, family, children, pets, plants, beauty, life). Similarly, most spiritual approaches to life encourage adherents to live simply but abundantly, through a posture of patient and humble acceptance, love and joy, unselfish service to others and gentle obedience to spiritual dictates, and to receive in turn the many blessings (including health?) of the spiritually directed life.

But what is the effect of this modification of at least surface spirituality? The follow-up data through four and a half years on this intervention project (Friedman et al., 1984; Thoresen, 1987) indicate that a significant reduction in coronary morbidity and mortality (as great as 50%) could be attributed to their training, and that this improvement did not occur in a comparable cardiac counseling group that did not receive the spiritual/behavior modification components. The investigators were quick to point out that most of the nearly threefold coronary risk reduction occurred in those with less advanced coronary disease. The fact that there was minimal risk reduction in those with advanced CHD suggests the importance of reaching these individuals before it is too late (i.e., before their "hearts are hardened" as warned repeatedly in biblical texts[6]). We wonder, given the strong spiritual coloring of the Type A modification program, if there was a differential effect on risk reduction as a function of the depth of the spiritual changes and/or the degree of the patient's faith (e.g., belief in God). Unfortunately, and as indicated earlier, to determine the answer to this very legitimate empirical question requires a sophistication in measurement that may not currently exist.

Although not specifically targeted by the Mt. Zion/Stanford Type A intervention of Friedman, Thoresen, Powell, and colleagues, another spiritual practice that may combat the world's pull toward workaholism and Type A Behavior is that of time out for worship, prayer, and spiritually mediated rest. We have already discussed the potential emotional, physical, and psychological benefits of relaxation through prayer. Another important component of spiritual practice is the prescribed day or time of rest. For Jewish and Christian adherents, the Sabbath and other religious holidays occur regularly enough to slow the body and mind down to refresh and restore, to worship God, commune with family and fellow believers, and recharge for the next period of work. The Judeo-Christian faiths, at least historically if not currently, are replete with examples of commanded and modeled rest and recreation. For example, one can point to the biblical commands to the Israelites that they "Be still and know that I am God" (Psalms 46:10), and to "Cease your striving"—powerful anti-Type A messages, indeed. Another biblical example (and, for that matter, model) of this type of message is the reporting of Jesus sleeping in the boat during the violent storm, gently rebuking his disciples for their fearful reactions (Mark 4); Jesus also enjoyed time with friends and at the eating table (Luke 10), and not working through or during meals. Importantly, Christians are called to "become like Jesus," arguably one of the best living examples of non-Type A functioning. A similar comment might be made about Buddha and Lao Tzu, as spiritual leaders seemingly consistent with our model definition.

The social, economic, and personal ravages of continual work were certainly evident (at least in retrospect) during the industrial revolution in England in the eighteenth century. In stark contrast to this materialistic all-work ethic stood the Church. Even today, the healthful, worshipful, and fellowship functions of the church's rest ethic is distorted both within and without the church. (We are distinguishing here between the church, which has been known to distort and misapply spiritual dictates and practices, and spirituality as we have defined and are speaking of in this chapter.) Their edicts regarding what is and what is not allowed on these holidays and days of rest is specifically stated, although not always closely adhered to or scrutinized.

Consistent with this, in the Friedman and Thoresen studies and programs, rest and recreation had to be specifically targeted for change. These researchers cautioned, however, that the Type A individual is likely to approach spiritual practices with characteristic "joyless striving." Thus special training and vigilance in monitoring are necessary to ensure that they are truly learning alternative, frequently the opposite (i.e., spiritual) approaches to living and working.

A clinical example. To illustrate the problem of altering the Type A approach to spiritual and nonspiritual activities, one of us (J. M.) has had several Type A "precoronary" patients in our hypertension clinic at the Jackson, Mississippi, VA Medical Center. Upon learning that the men were churchgoers, and involved in every committee and function imaginable in their church or synagogue, we introduced the rationale that the patients needed "spiritual feeding" more than they needed one more place to perform, and that perhaps their God wants them to be filled and healthy and at peace . . . that God even (lovingly) commands this (see Miller's case example in Chapter 4). On the latter point, scriptural and religious documentation is then produced to back up this claim. Upon receiving the patients' agreement for slowing down as a *spiritual goal* as well as a health goal, we proceed systematically to program into their daily lives the prayer, meditation, worship time, rest, and loving time with family that are clearly prescribed by their religion. In this way, their rule-governed (belief-mediated) behavior system is tapped, to lay the foundation better and to enhance the effectiveness of the primary behavioral contingency-management therapy deemed necessary to change their health and disease risk behaviors. Not only is this dual approach well received by the patients as being highly consistent with their spiritual belief systems, but it also tends to result in significant social, emotional, and spiritual support from wives and significant others who share the same faith. Importantly, active, positive social support in the home environment has been shown to be one of the most critical components for the maintenance of health behavior/life-style change (Brownell, Marlatt, Lichtenstein, & Wilson, 1986; Martin & Dubbert, 1982).

Self-Absorption, Depression, and the Need to Control: Additional Coronary/Health Risk Factors?

At the core of the coronary-prone behavior pattern rest the related concepts of personal control and self-absorption, as illustrated in the previous sections and the case example. We are intrigued with recent findings that Type As appear to be locked into obsessive and exaggerated efforts to control even the most uncontrollable aspects of their environments (Glass, 1977), and that Type As, as well as clinically depressed individuals, engage in significantly more self-referencing (highly frequent use of personal pronouns *I*, *my*, and so on), and are said to be "self-absorbed," possibly even at the expense of others as well as accurate perceptions of themselves and their world (Friedman & Rosenman, 1974; Friedman et al., 1984; Scherwitz et al., 1978; Scherwitz et al., 1986). As indicated previously, this pattern of narcissistic, often depressive self-absorption has been identified as a significant coronary risk factor (Scherwitz et al., 1986; Scherwitz et al., 1978), as well as a general mental and physical health risk factor (Booth-Kewley & Friedman, 1987; Ingram, 1987). Intimately characteristic of both the Type A and the depressive is obsessive overcontrolling of self and others, often resulting in despair and further depression at their failure to do so (perfectly). Not surprisingly, many Type As are clinically depressed (Booth-Kewley & Friedman, 1987), especially later on in life after years of this fearful, wrenching struggle (Thoresen, 1987). Recall that these patterns of fearful overcontrolling and self-absorption stand in stark contrast to the spiritually oriented life-style as we have defined it.[7]

There may also be cultural differences that characterize individuals' approach to relating to and controlling others and their world, particularly one's family and job (Thoresen, 1987; Weisz, Rothbaum, & Blackburn, 1984). These basic styles may translate into some essential differences in health and happiness. For example, in the Japanese culture, there are clearer and more consistent sex role differentiations, closer family ties, and more of a cooperative spirit in home and work relationships, whereas in the Western (especially American) culture, the family roles are more confused, family ties are more distant, and nonfamily relationships are characterized by a much more highly individualized and competitive spirit, both in and out of the work environment (Weisz, Rothbaum, & Blackburn, 1984; Thoresen, 1987).

Significantly, these basic life-styles, when compared epidemiologically, have shown lower CHD risks in the Japanese who have relocated to American and adopted our high cholesterol diet in spite of the fact that they may have consequently developed hypercholesterolemia (Thoresen, 1987).

A number of spiritual systems would seem to encourage a less community-oriented, if not lonely self-oriented pursuit, such as may be found in many Eastern religions. Even classical Christianity (Foster, 1978) may be partially vulnerable to this argument. Yet, formal spiritual and religious disciplines almost always embrace the goal of self-surrender (to God, to a higher power of spirit) or the ultimate achievement of selflessness. Christians, for example, speak of denying or crucifying the self and the ego, while Zen Buddhists attempt to achieve total oneness with the universe through complete material sacrifice and spiritual self-loss (e.g., Hesse, 1951). The spiritual practice of regularly offering and surrendering one's self, and relinquishing its constant companions of unreasonable expectations and super "rights" (e.g., to always be right; to complete and constant "success," "fame," "fortune," comfort, and so on) may in fact be an exceptionally worthy physical health goal, and not just mental and spiritual health goals. At least from the preliminary data standpoint, this would appear to be a moderately substantiated path to greater health, though the best approach to becoming more spiritual has been debated without benefit of modern scientific inquiry for centuries. Might, then, the ever growing (in both quantity and quality) data base in the coming years help to shine some light on this question? We believe and hope so.

Expectancy, Placebo Effect, and Faith: A Surrender to Health?

The mistrusting, insecure, and hypercontrolling pattern, so character-istic of Westernized Type As, may be viewed as just the opposite of the type of individual most likely to benefit from even inert medical and psychological therapies. In research on coronary patients enrolled in exercise rehabilitation programs, some studies found that Type As had higher dropout rates than others (Martin & Dubbert, 1982). Indeed, most therapy regimens require a degree of trust, faith, and positive expectancy (particular problems with the Type As we have been discussing; Powell & Thoresen, 1987; Williams, 1984) for them to be optimally effective.

We know that many who fail to respond to treatment do so because (a) they never come for treatment, (b) they fail to comply adequately when they do, and/or (c) they have a negative outcome expectancy (DiMatteo & DiNicola, 1982; Haynes, Taylor, & Sackett, 1979). Refusal to undergo treatment, poor to incorrect adherence, and inadequate faith or belief in the treatment are all interrelated causes for treatment and health change failures. Each of these levels of treatment effectiveness/breakdown may be seen to relate, in turn, to the spiritual processes of acceptance, surrender, trust, belief, submission, and obedience (to a higher authority or power). Might it be that the spiritual aspects of therapeutic control and effectiveness constitute a critical component, as is apparent in the Type A pattern and treatment?

Let's take the case of the so-called placebo effect, the nonspecific therapeutic effect, or "faith-healing" (choose a label, depending on your spiritual stance). To occur, this nonspecific, or belief-mediated, benefit would appear to require at a minimum that the patient surrender (at least temporarily) control to the therapeutic agent or vehicle (i.e., take the treatment). Treatments with more marginal efficacy might further necessitate relinquishment of significant doubt, skepticism, or cynicism toward the therapeutic process and delivery agent, while assuming the attitude of expectation or faith in a specific positive outcome associated with the intervention or intervener.

There is considerable literature, especially in the fields of psychology and medicine, on the "art" of healing, and the importance of the health care provider capitalizing on the patient's expectancy for and belief in the efficacy of treatment—particularly when the treatment leaves something to be desired in regard to its potency, specificity, duration, and/or generality (see DiMatteo & DiNocola, 1982, for an excellent discussion of this). Assuming the vital role of these "nonspecific" factors in ensuring positive outcome, might it then be predicted (a) that those most susceptible to optimal treatment contact and benefit will possess a more complete trust or belief, and higher positive expectancy, in the treatment and the health care provider; (b) that, on the whole, these optimal compliers and responders will be patients who have the more deeply rooted belief or faith, and possibly spiritual orientation to a higher power; and (c) that these same individuals would show the most enhanced treatment effectiveness across a variety of clinical interventions, perhaps especially for those treatments that have in the past demonstrated the most variable results (e.g., hypnosis, vitamin or nutritional therapy, relaxation, prayer, experimental drugs, biofeedback)?

These are certainly testable hypotheses, but at least for the latter two (b and c) we must rely on our currently unidimensional ability to assess this spiritually (note our previous section on the problems of measurement). Further, in any test of this sort, we must also acknowledge and incorporate the important recent advances in our understanding of cognitive processes (Bandura, 1986), especially as perception and cognitive processes relate to pathophysiological processes, health optimization, and healing.

In the behavioral medicine arena, treatment efficacy research provides further indications of the potential importance of cognitive and belief factors to health and healing (Bandura, 1986; Meichenbaum & Jaremko, 1983). While the holistic health movement has helped to promulgate the notion of "mind power" over illness, with intriguing anecdotal case studies (e.g., Brown, 1985; Segal, 1986), these offerings have been disappointing from a scientific standpoint in that they have not stood up to careful epidemiologic and laboratory scrutiny. Yet, there would appear to be some reason to consider the importance of belief and expectation to the treatment of specific disorders even from a stricter scientific stance. For example, Andrasik and Holroyd (1980), in a study on cognitive control of headache pain, found that biofeedback for reducing frontalis EMG (the current nondrug treatment of choice for muscle-contraction headaches, along with relaxation) was no better than biofeedback for increasing muscle tension when paired with instructions that increased positive expectations for success. The belief or expectation that this otherwise counterproductive therapy (increasing muscle tension theoretically should have increased the headache and pain reports) was as powerful or more powerful than the therapeutic change attributable to reductions in muscle tension per se; and it is unlikely that the headaches were cognitive distortions merely relabeled.

Another example of the importance of faith and belief to health outcome comes from studies on coronary patients who were admitted to the hospital in acute distress (angina, myocardial infarction). Those who did not give in to anxiety and alarm, presumably due at least in part to a belief in the ability of the medical people to treat or heal them effectively (as well as some denial of the life-threatening nature of their cardiac symptoms), encountered fewer medical complications (including death) during the critical first few days, than those who were highly fearful (and presumably less trusting in the medical treatment) (Gentry & Williams, 1975). Unfortunately, this belief, or denial, may be subsequently associated with noncompliance to the cardiac rehabilitation regimen. While measures of spirituality or religious faith were apparently not obtained, we wonder if that subset of patients who were less acutely fearful and yet more compliant with the longer-term medical and health regimen consisted of the patients who had a more solidly established spiritual orientation to living and, maybe more important, relatively less fear of death because of an abiding faith in an afterlife? We hope these data might be collected in future investigations of this sort.

Approaching this from a different angle, it may be that the more spiritually, or religiously, oriented may be more likely to surrender their skepticism, cynicism, or overall resistance to efforts to "control" them (so apparent in Type A) likely to interfere with compliance to regimens prescribed by health care providers in positions of natural authority (i.e., physician, nurse, psychologist, dentist). The Judeo-Christian and many Eastern spiritual systems typically exhort their adherents to submit lovingly and trustingly to (God-ordained) authorities, rather than fight against them, while retaining faith all the while that God or a higher power or spirit, who ultimately controls the authorities, will not let them come to harm.[8] Surrender to health in this sense may also encompass surrendering notions of bodily immortality and seeking medical and health treatment at even the first sign of early warning symptoms. A spiritual orientation may in fact enhance this sensitivity and openness to seeking appropriate help, independent of one's health locus of control (though a key exception would be religious sects such as Christian Scientists, Jehovah's Witnesses, and perhaps some Pentecostals, who believe so strongly in faith healing that they refuse even supplemental medical care, blood transfusions, and so on). Indeed, this relinquishment or surrender of at least some personal control, even temporarily, would seem a necessary element to all effective therapeutic interventions, whether it be to a drug, to instructions of a health care provider, or to a spiritual leader or scripture.

Along these lines, an exciting and otherwise unexplainable body of research comes from the secondary investigations, following several major clinical trials, of the independent effects of compliance on therapeutic outcome (Epstein, 1984). For example, even the act of "faithful" compliance to a nonactive placebo drug regimen has been associated with therapeutic effects, sometimes even equivalent to a known efficacious drug (Epstein, 1984). In a startling example of this "unexplainable" phenomena, the Coronary Drug Project Research Group (1980) found no differences in coronary mortality across 3789 post-myocardial infarction (MI) patients randomized to either a placebo drug or a highly potent drug (clofibrate) now known to lower blood cholesterol and associated mortality. There was, however, a significant lowering of mortality effect for compliance, independent of whether they complied with the active drug or the inert placebo. Several other major studies in the health treatment areas of cancer (Pizzo, Robichaud, Edwards, Schumaker, Kramer, & Johnson, 1983) and alcoholism (Fuller, Roth, & Long, 1983) had very similar results; that is, treatment effects that were compliance-mediated and not related to active drug versus placebo use.

These data on the nonspecific (or perhaps even highly specific, though currently unmeasurable) effects of belief or expectancy on the actual medication efficacy may be framed in a number of different ways. One alternative explanation might be that compliance to other facets of the therapy may have improved along with the expectancy and pill compliance, though no data were available to confirm or refute this interpretation. Another alternative explanation that we believe is worthy of scientific evaluation would point to the profound biopsychosocial "normalizing"(healing) that might accrue to spiritually mediated exercises of faith. For example, this might include the surrender of control and (therapeutic) resistance and the mobilization of the more centrally mediated natural healing mechanisms such as natural killer cells and so on—our God-given biological forces against disease, if you will (the final section in the chapter concerns this very mechanism, the immune system, and its susceptibility and sensitivity to things spiritual). The case studies provided in the following section help to illustrate the importance of this basic relinquishment of resistance to therapeutic intervention—perhaps the least of the potential benefits that may accrue from tailoring the treatment to fit and capitalizing upon the individual's spiritual/faith system.

Finally, while the whole area of "faith healing" is replete with countless unsubstantiated claims, there are some intriguing connections between faithful prayer and worship and physical and psychological healing. For example, Glik (1985) found in a large study in Baltimore that devout Christian (Charismatic) pray-ers (n = 93) and Eastern spiritualists who believed in and practiced healing prayer (n = 93) had significantly more positive scores on wellness measures than a control group of individuals (n = 137) who were regular users of primary care, even when sex, age, marital status, illness severity, religiosity, and participation rates were controlled statistically. More systematic and carefully controlled scientific inquiry is needed in this whole area of faith healing, especially to attempt to isolate the independent factors (if any) responsible for or associated with the "healing" or health improvement.

It is at this point that our focus will shift to an arena hinted at in several places earlier. It is in some ways the most fascinating of all, and it has only become possible through very recent advances in a physiological measurement technology developed mainly by cancer researchers. What better place to study disease processes and psychosocial, behavioral, and especially spiritual connections to health and disease than in the body's natural mechanisms of defense against disease and infection—the immune system.

Love, Spirituality, and Health:
The Immune System

Several years ago, a distinguished psychology professor from Harvard, David McClelland, reported on a most interesting series of experiments conducted in his laboratory (McClelland, 1985). In these experiments, instead of taking the usual approach of either inducing stress in the laboratory, or of finding individuals suffering from very high stress or a stress-related disorder, McClelland and his associates attempted to produce the most positive feeling or experience possible, and observe what would happen to the body's immune system. Recent research (Kiecolt-Glaser, 1986; Kiecolt-Glaser & Glaser, 1987) had clearly indicated the role of stress in interrupting healthy immune function, but little or nothing had been done on the positive side of that equation—whether the function of the immune system would be enhanced by "healthy" or optimal emotions or experiences. Deciding that feelings of love constituted the highest and best human feeling, they showed a film to a series of subjects depicting two adolescents in love. Surprising to them, no consistent improvement in natural killer (NK) T-cell activity could be found (it actually decreased in some), even in the many who reported they had very positive feelings about the film. The second experiment was the most fascinating: McClelland then obtained a film of Mother Theresa, the Nobel laureate missionary nun, describing her work, her life, her people, and her God of love. McClelland and co-workers labeled "Divine Love" what was so profoundly represented by Mother Theresa in this film and so experienced by the viewers of the film (later changed to "Div. Love," and then to "selfless love" so as not to upset the nonreligious; McClelland, 1985; McKay, personal communication, September 12, 1986).

The results were dramatic. While only half of the subjects reported liking the film and being positively affected by it, all showed a significant improvement in immunofunction, as measured by salivary natural killer cell activity. Several replications and follow-up studies with more substantial immune function measures have now been conducted (McKay, personal communication), with highly consistent results. While the earlier measure of immunofunction (salivary IgA) used in their initial studies is considered by many to be one of the least reliable measures (due, in part, to the variations in salivary concentrations of NK cells as a function of dry versus wet mouths), McClelland's data are provocative, and worthy of further exploration.

In another interesting area of research on psychosocial (and spiritual) moderators of immune function, a variety of stress-related predicaments and reactions, including generalized depression, troubled relationships, and particularly marital separation and divorce, have been closely tied to negative health effects and, in some more recent studies, significant immunosuppression. For example, increased incidence of cancer has been linked to chronic and intense emotional distress, both anecdotally (Segal, 1986) and experimentally (Kiecolt-Glaser & Glaser, 1987). In one fascinating study, it was found that more depressed in-patients had significantly poorer repair of damaged DNA (a common precursor of the development of cancer following exposure to carcinogens) (Kiecolt-Glaser & Glaser, 1987). Depression, as opposed to time-limited grieving and controlled letting out of emotionality, can be viewed as a joyless isolation that is counter to the teachings of many spiritual and religious systems.

In another study of the psychoimmunology of stress and depression, Glaser, Kiecolt-Glaser, Speicher, and Holliday (1985) studied medical students' exposure to three life-quality-impairing viruses, Epstein-Barr virus (EBV), Herpes simplex I, and cytomegalovirus. When they separated groups on the basis of relative loneliness, they found something striking: Subjects who scored higher on the (UCLA) loneliness scale had significantly higher EBV antibody counts (suggesting greater exposure and immunocompromise), while those scoring the lowest on loneliness showed significantly lower increases in all three virus antibodies to examination stress than the higher scorers.[9]

Expanding their scope of inquiry to the marital relationship, Kiecolt-Glaser (1986) and her colleagues (Kiecolt-Glaser, Fisher, Oqrocki et al., in press), and others (Jasnoski, 1986), have also found that, among married subjects, poorer marital quality is associated with greater depression and a poorer response on three qualitative measures of immune function. This same health decrement was also found up to a year following separation and/or divorce, but not in those whose relationships and marriages were generally untroubled. In their review of this body of evidence, Kiecolt-Glaser and Glaser (1987) point out that marital disruption is generally associated with significantly compromised immunofunction, and, consequently, disease and infection, and that, among divorced persons, there are six times the number of deaths, for example, from pneumonia. As indicated previously, love, marriage, and fidelity are main tenets of most spiritual systems, and violating them causes anxiety, "troubled hearts", spiritual and psychological pain, and apparently some rather major health compromises. It may, therefore, be that the spirituality of lovingness, fidelity, forgiveness, and attitude of surrender (i.e., to a higher power other than self), as well as peace and rest, common to so many spiritual systems, provides an essential framework for health optimization and disease prevention, and that this "inoculation" has profound biological bases. Yet, further study is certainly warranted before conclusions can be drawn as to the potential protectiveness of these spiritual practices and attitudes.

We have discussed to this point the "what" and the "why" of integrating spiritual principles, practices, and life-styles with health psychology. In the final section of the chapter, we will attempt to illustrate briefly the "how" of this integration of these two seemingly incompatible approaches to improving health and well-being.

Health Spirituality in Action: Case Studies

Spiritual Approaches to Health Program Adherence

Over the past 10 years or so, our (particularly J. M.'s) research has included investigating strategies for enhancing adherence to prescribed or desired health behaviors. Frequently, these health promotion programs involved increasing exercise behavior (Martin & Dubbert,

1982, 1984) and/or decreasing or eliminating cigarette (Prue, Davis, Martin, & Moss, 1983) and alcohol consumption. In some cases, we have met with particular resistance to change and have consequently searched for supplemental or alternative interventions to our more standard behavioral armamentarium. One of the more effective supplemental procedures, when it has been attempted, has been the use of spiritual approaches in those religiously committed resistors. Several examples from our clinical research serve to illustrate this point.

Smoking. In the summer of 1985 and again in the spring of 1986, several colleagues (J. Fitterling, W. R. Richter, J. Fowler) and I offered a smoking treatment program to recovering alcoholics who had at least one year of sobriety and were all active members of Alcoholics Anonymous (a number were alcoholism treatment counselors at local hospitals). Most had smoked two or more packs per day of high tar and nicotine cigarettes for most of their lives, admitted to being highly dependent on nicotine, and had requested our assistance due to increasing health problems associated with their smoking. Although the program was especially tailored to minimize the pain and punishment of withdrawal, between 25% and 50% of the individuals had extreme difficulty with certain components of the treatment and were non-compliant and resistant to any further or alternate steps. Also, these individuals were frequently a disruptive influence in the group treatment sessions, arguing against many of the suggestions and vocally disputing the effectiveness of many of the treatment components. It was no secret to any of us or to the other group members that these were the ones who were not going to make it, and we felt helpless to prevent their imminent failure in the program. In a last-ditch effort to turn around these highly resistant, likely dropouts, we recommended attacking the dependence on spiritual as well as behavioral grounds.

In our desperation with the rapidly failing group, we agreed we had little or nothing to lose given the high degree of noncompliance and struggle exhibited by the smokers, who were then a couple weeks into the 12-week program. We felt that shifting to an approach that included tapping into their previous successful spiritual experience in AA was worth the risk of alienating those wanting a pure "scientific" approach, because most of the smokers believed in God and had achieved and maintained their sobriety through spiritual/behavioral steps (i.e., AA 12-Step Program; Alcoholics Anonymous, 1976). We encouraged giving up control to God, praying for deliverance from the habit, and praying for success for each other, while also following the behavioral steps of the program. This suggestion met with wide approval, and we held discussions each week on their spiritual progress, prayer effectiveness, and spiritual homework assignments (e.g., break urge-smoke behavioral chain by giving each urge or compulsion to God in a brief prayer, followed by leaving the situation). Significantly, none of these high probability, highly resistant smokers dropped out, and the majority were able successfully to quit. Interestingly, even the individuals who had been the most upset and outspoken came to subsequent sessions with a peace and quietness that we had trouble explaining in scientific terms. In social learning terms, it had made sense for us to tap into a system that had previously been successful for them, and that was consonant with their spiritual beliefs and practices.

Exercise adherence. In working with many of the individuals who requested help in initiating and maintaining a regular exercise program, we would often come across those for whom none of our behavioral procedures seemed to work. In one particular case, a young mother of two with two jobs was losing her battle against being overweight. She approached me for help in exercising. She had tried many of the behavioral techniques we would normally suggest (see Martin & Dubbert, 1984), and none seemed to help much until I asked her if she had ever prayed about it (I had been aware she was a religiously committed person). She had not. She had tried most everything else, without success, and was reluctant to attempt behavioral techniques that had previously been unsuccessful. She had particular difficulty fitting exercise into a very busy day; we discussed morning exercise as one way to be sure to fit it in, but she admitted total failure with arising in time. After making other unsuccessful recommendations, I suggested she, perhaps even as a test of her faith, take the following steps: (a) admit that, on her own at least, she just didn't currently have the "power" or motivation to get up and exercise; (b) pray at night for God to help her arise in time and have the desire to go exercise; (c) completely turn the outcome over to God after praying and putting the matter in God's hands; and *then* (d) follow the previously tried behavioral techniques that had not helped (i.e., contracting with loved one, posting exercise graph, laying exercise clothes out night before, making public declarations of intent to exercise, and so on). Shortly thereafter, I remember her coming to me excitedly to tell me that it was working. At the very least, this spiritually oriented action served to lower or eliminate her resistance to change for a time, such that she had enough contact with the behavioral intervention package and contingencies that they could strengthen her exercise behavior in that critical early acquisition stage.

Needle phobia and cancer. A final illustration of the adjunct use of spiritually oriented approaches to improving health behavior or lowering therapeutic resistance concerns a terminal brain cancer patient we saw on request of the hospital out-patient cancer treatment program (Cole & Martin, 1986). Over the past number of months, this male patient had refused to allow blood samples or any needle puncture following a traumatic episode of blood transfusion a few years earlier. The physicians felt his irradiated tumor was returning (the headaches were coming back at an alarming rate) and wanted to conduct more tests that required blood samples and venous dye—all involving needle puncture. We attempted relaxation and desensitization with this needle phobic, but he was so sensitized that he would bolt out of the room at the first presentation of phobic material. He refused a chemical relaxant (e.g., Valium), when we suggested that would help him in the early stages of the desensitization, while denying the seriousness of his condition to his family and others. He and his very concerned family were all religiously committed, and so the first session with the patient and family revolved around the meaning of death and suffering, from the standpoint of their faith, and the importance of submitting to (medical) "authorities" as an act of obedience to God. The family was encouraged to pray and talk together as much as possible about his condition and the tests and treatment. When we suggested a special method of relaxing him (exercising to exhaustion on a treadmill to prevent physiological over-arousal), followed by an immediate blood sample, all the while the family was praying for him in the hospital chapel, he and the family agreed. The family and hospital staff worked together, with everyone having an important role. The spiritual-behavioral intervention was a success: He allowed the needle puncture/ blood sample with no anxiety or avoidance both then and over subsequent clinic visits. Though the treatment was confounded, and there is no way to know which were the active ingredients, we believe the patient and his family may not have let us attempt the exercise-mediated relaxation and desensitization (actually it was probably more a flooding/exhaustion paradigm) had we not also approached them from an adjunct spiritual orientation. This case is another example of the social support and reduction of therapeutic resistance that a spiritual "assist" can bring about in families who are religiously committed.

Summary and Conclusions

The present chapter has provided a relatively broad-based review of the spiritual aspects of the field of health psychology/behavioral medicine. It has explored the spirituality-health interface through some relatively recent and provocative research and practical findings that relate to spirituality and health. A somewhat select sample of supportive research was presented, however, for two reasons. First, we believe, along with some others (Rosenhan, 1987), that there has been a significant bias against objectively presenting and fairly discussing, much less publishing in reputable journals, this body of evidence in the scientific (especially psychology) community. We chose here to provide a counterbalancing overview of the positive side of these findings and associations. Second, due to space considerations and the relative lack of studies fairly investigating spiritual influences on health, we chose to direct our chapter to the evidence in support of the possibility that factors and procedures commonly labeled spiritual may have an important impact on health. Indeed, one of our primary goals has been to provide a heuristic for additional, much needed follow-up research.

We appreciate the problems inherent in this sort of a "quasi-scientific" venture with regard to defining and quantifying "spirituality" to the satisfaction of both the religious and the secular scientific communities. We also are aware of both the importance and the difficulty of differentiating religious from nonreligious (or theistic from nontheistic) spirituality, and the relative efficacy of each in predicting and promoting health. Indeed, can we differentiate between the appearance of spirituality and the true practice of spirituality? That is, will it be possible in our studies to penetrate the cloak of spiritual talk and motion in those who are not truly spiritual and to uncover the core spirituality embedded in those persons who live genuinely in accord with the spiritual principles and practices we have discussed? Certainly, there are many alternative explanations for the apparent effects of prayer, faith/belief, spiritual fellowship, and adherence to spiritual dictates and conduct of behavior and thought on health behavior and disease inoculation and control. Nevertheless, there is much to be learned and we cannot nor should not discount spiritually oriented life-style as a viable (and perhaps superior to some) avenue to health acquisition and maintenance.

Along these lines, we (and we hope you) found it fascinating that so many of the spiritual prescriptions and proscriptions that greatly predate modern medical and biobehavioral science relate to disease prevention and control, as well as quality of life. The diseases and health disorders caused by or associated with social, behavioral, and emotional disregulation, as well as overconsumption, are our most important health problems today and we can little afford to ignore potentially significant associations with realms of experience that may not currently be directly observable.

There are several conclusions and interpretations that we felt can be drawn from what has been discussed here. First, the research we have presented suggests, in some cases quite strongly, that certain health problems may be related to deficits or excesses that might be termed *spiritual*, and that optimal health may require a spiritual as well as a social, behavioral, and physical homeostasis. Second, a number of health-improvement interventions can easily be characterized as spiritual, and these seem to have promising impact on the fields of health psychology and theology. Third, health issues raise spiritual questions and matters that have been recognized for millennia. Fourth, many clients view the world and themselves through spiritual eyes, and their behavior-guiding religious and spiritual arenas overlap nicely—especially so in health psychology.

We believe the associations between spirituality and health are worthy of much more attention then they have received even to this point. Three actions are suggested: first, that we take a far more comprehensive and scientific look at the connection between spiritual practices and health. This is an area in need of further scientific inquiry, especially to understand more about how the mind-body and "spirit" (however defined) interact. Second, the spiritual community should become more aware of the more clearly documented negative and positive health consequences of behaviors and thought patterns that are consistent with spiritual and unspiritual life-styles.

Finally, acknowledging that most of our clients and patients believe in God (Bergin, 1980; Princeton Religion Research Center, 1986; Rosenhan, 1987), and understanding that many of them are deeply spiritual, we believe it is important for clinicians and clinical scientists to understand when and how best to treat the "whole" person who comes replete with risk factors, disease, and other forms of suffering. Can we as clinicians and health behavior change agents really do the best job possible if we fail to explore, understand, and possibly utilize the spiritual dimension of our clients? It is noteworthy that rule-governed behavior can be much more powerful and resistant to extinction than contingency-governed behavior, and that, whenever possible, health clinicians should connect their secular prescriptions and proscriptions for health with the individual's spiritual belief system. We emphasize the importance and desirability of combining modern, well-tested medical and behavioral health interventions with appropriate spiritual approaches (some of which we have presented here). We do not condone the reliance on spiritual methods to the exclusion of needed medical and psychological care, but rather that they be used concurrently for willing individuals—a tack we believe is consistent with Jewish, Christian, and other spiritual traditions, and that should enhance rather than diminish the effectiveness of the more scientifically accepted secular approaches. Other chapters in the volume speak much more eloquently to the importance of this. In order to ensure compliance to our health regimens, it may be necessary (or it may greatly help) to convince the spiritually minded individual that it is important (if not commanded) that they adhere to their spiritual proscriptions and prescriptions, *and* that this has been shown to be associated with better health and quality of life.

We hope the reader's appetite has been whetted and that this chapter and volume will lead to further exploration of the most fascinating common ground between health psychology, behavior therapy, and spiritual walks of life. The connection cannot and should not be ignored. We also hope that more and better research will be conducted on this vital topic, and that health professionals will continue to discover that the principal difference between treatment of part of the person and healing of the whole person may be as much a spiritual-behavioral formula as anything else.

NOTES

1. Some preliminary data from the *mental health* arena are suggestive of the importance, in certain individuals and contexts, of a spiritual orientation and approach to stress coping. For example, Lewis and Lewis (1985) found that religious clients were rated by therapists as requiring significantly fewer therapy sessions than their nonreligious counterparts, independent of whether the therapist was religious or not; while Propst (1980) reported the superiority of religious over nonreligious imagery in treating mildly depressed religious clients (remember that most clients come to psychologists and physicians with a belief in God). In addition, a reportedly effective spiritual psychotherapy from Japan, "Morita therapy," incorporates isolation and meditation, reading of spiritual literature, and the spiritual step of surrendering resistance and struggle against symptoms such as anxiety, with progressive physical activity and verbal therapy (Miura & Usa, 1970; cited in Weisz, Rothbaum, & Blackburn, 1984).

2. In this regard, a 2000-year-old exhortation from the Bible is attributed to Jesus, who warned: "Who of you by worrying can add a single hour to his life?" (Matthew 6:27; NIV).

3. The definition of "peace" from the Christian perspective, for example, takes on a much more profound meaning than mere relaxation, as "the *peace* of God, which transcends all understanding, will guard your hearts and your minds" (Philippians 4:7; NIV).

4. Example prescriptions relating to this occur throughout the Bible (i.e., "Whenever two or three are gathered together in my name . . . it is not good to be alone . . . feed my sheep . . . confess your sins one to another and be healed").

5. This exercise parallels closely another example from the Bible, namely Jesus' exhortation to his disciples to be last (and thereby become "first" in God's eyes), to seat themselves at the end of the table, in the most humble position, rather than at the head—to follow Jesus' example of humble patience and putting others first (certainly the opposite of Type A Behavior!). On the surface, it seems almost paradoxical when Jesus says "the last shall be first," or "the meek shall inherit the earth," until one considers these statements in the context of living a long, happy, and fruitful life through humble and patient (and healthy) low-stress days and years.

6. Though these religious scriptures refer more to a behavior of stubbornness, self-will, hostile refusal to submit to God's will and authority, pride, and arrogance in portraying a "hardened heart," could it be that these same behaviors, when carried to the extreme (and in a Type A fashion) also contribute to a hardening of the coronary arteries and eventually a "killing" of the heart (i.e., through tissue damage to the heart muscle due to a nonfatal or fatal myocardial infarction), as might likely occur in the Type A with more advanced CHD?

7. In fact, preliminary evidence suggests that if and when this pattern changes to less self-absorption and more outward relating to the world (e.g., after cognitive therapy for depression, Type A modification therapy, religious conversion, healing prayer), both mental and physical health tend to improve, although the isolation of this benefit is confounded by the fact that the converse may also be true—completing a bidirectional interaction, that is, when a person gets healthier mentally and physically, he or she becomes less depressed and more social (and perhaps more spiritual and loving?).

8. From the Bible, we find this comforting psalm: "The Lord who watches over you will not slumber. . . . The Lord will keep you from all harm . . . both now and forevermore" (Psalm 121; NIV).

9. Again, Jewish teachings caution: "It is not good to be alone" (Genesis 2:18). Perhaps this ancient warning referred not just to the dampening of emotional and sexual fulfillment but also to the potential negative health consequences (e.g., cancer) accruing to the lonely life.

REFERENCES

Alcoholics Anonymous. (1976). *Alcoholics Anonymous "Big Book"* (3rd ed.). New York: AA World Services.

Allport, G. W. (1954). *The nature of prejudice.* Reading, MA: Addison-Wesley.

Allport, G. W., & Ross, J. M. (1967). Personal religious orientation and prejudice. *Journal of Personality and Social Psychology, 5,* 432-443.

Andrasik, F., & Holroyd, K. A. (1980). A test of specific and nonspecific effects in the biofeedback treatment of tension headache. *Journal of Consulting and Clinical Psychology, 48*, 575-586.

Antonovsky, A. (1979). *Health, stress and coping.* San Francisco: Jossey-Bass.

Bandura, A. (1986). *Social foundations of thought & action: A social cognitive theory.* Englewood Cliffs, NJ: Prentice-Hall.

Baum, A., Grunberg, N. E., & Singer, J. E. (1982). The use of psychological and neuroendocrinological measurements in the study of stress. *Health Psychology, 1*, 217-236.

Behavioral Medicine Update. (1984). Cardiovascular reactivity [Special issue]. *6*, 7-33.

Bergin, A. (1980). Psychotherapy and religious values. *Journal of Consulting and Clinical Psychology, 48*, 95-105.

Berkman, L. F., & Breslow, L. (1983). *Health and ways of living: The Alameda County Study.* Oxford: Oxford University Press.

Berkman, L. F., & Syme, S. L. (1979). Social networks, host resistance, and mortality: A nine-year follow-up study of Alameda County residents. *American Journal of Epidemiology, 109*, 186-204.

The Bible. (1978). New International Version (NIV). Grand Rapids, MI: Zondervan.

Blumenthal, J. A., Williams, R. B., & Kong, Y. (1978). Type A behavior pattern and coronary atherosclerosis. *Circulation, 58*, 634-639.

Booth-Kewley, S., & Friedman, H. S. (1987). Psychological predictors of heart disease: A quantitative review. *Psychological Bulletin, 101*, 343-362.

Brown, M. (1985, November). The psychic search. *American Health,* pp. 64-70.

Brownell, K. D., Marlatt, G. A., Lichtenstein, E., & Wilson, G. T. (1986). Understanding and preventing relapse. *American Psychologist, 41*, 765-782.

Bruhn, J. G., Chandler, B., Miller, M. C., Wolf, S., & Lynn, T. N. (1966). Social aspects of coronary heart disease in two adjacent, ethnically different communities. *American Journal of Public Health, 55*, 1493-1506.

Bruhn, J. G., & Wolf, S. (1978). Update on Roseta, Pa.: Testing a prediction. *Psychosomatic Medicine, 40*, 86.

Byrd, R. C. (1984). Positive therapeutic effects of intercessory prayer in a coronary care unit population. *Circulation, 70*(Supp. 2), 212. (abstract)

Carlson, C. R., Bacaseta, P. & Simanton, D. (in press). A controlled comparison of devotional mediation and progressive relaxation. *Journal of Psychology and Theology.*

Chesney, A. P., & Gentry, W. D. (1982). Psychosocial factors mediating health risk: A balanced perspective. *Preventive Medicine, 11*, 612-617.

Chesney, A. P., & Rosenman, R. H. (Eds.). (1985). *Anger and hostility in cardiovascular and behavioral disorders.* New York: Hemisphere.

Cohen, S., & Syme, S. L. (Eds.). (1985). *Social support and health.* New York: Academic.

Cole, P., & Martin, J. E. (1986, November). *Exercise and the treatment of a simple phobia: A case study.* Paper presented before the Association for Advancement of Behavior Therapy, Chicago.

Comstock, G. W., Abbey, H., & Lundin, F. E. (1970). The nonofficial census as a basic tool for epidemiologic observations in Washington County, Maryland. In I. Kessler & M. Levin (Eds.), *The community as an epidemiologic laboratory* (pp. 73-97). Baltimore: Johns Hopkins University Press.

Comstock, G. W., & Partridge, K. P. (1972). Church attendance and health. *Journal of Chronic Diseases, 25*, 665-672.

Coronary Drug Project Research Group. (1980). Influence of adherence to treatment and response of cholesterol on mortality in the Coronary Drug Project. *New England Journal of Medicine, 303*, 1038-1041.

Datey, K. K., Deshmukh, S. N., Dalvi, C. P., & Vinekar, S. L. (1969). "Shavasan": A yogic exercise in the management of hypertension. *Angiology, 20*, 325-333.

DiMatteo, M. R., & DiNicola, D. D. (1982). *Achieving patient compliance.* New York: Pergamon.

Epstein, L. H. (1984). The direct effects of compliance on health outcome. *Health Psychology, 3*, 385-393.

Ellis, A. (1971). *The case against religion: A psychotherapist's view.* New York: Institute for Rational Living.

Ellis, A. (1980). Psychotherapy and atheistic values: A response to A. E. Bergin's "Psychotherapy and religious values." *Journal of Consulting and Clinical Psychology, 48*, 635-639.

Farquhar, J. W. (1979). *The American way of life need not be hazardous to your health.* New York: Norton.

Faulkner, J., & DeJong, G. (1966). Religiosity in 5-D: An empirical analysis. *Social Forces, 45*, 246-254.

Fishbein, M., & Ajzen, I. (1974). Attitudes toward objects as predictors of single and multiple behavioral criteria. *Psychological Review, 81*, 59-74.

Foster, R. (1978). *Celebration of discipline: The path to spiritual growth.* New York: Harper & Row.

Friedman, H. S., & Booth-Kewley, S. (1987). The "disease-prone personality": A meta-analytic view of the construct. *American Psychologist, 42*, 539-555.

Friedman, M. (1978). Modifying "Type A" behavior in heart attack patients. *Primary Cardiology, 1*, 9-13.

Friedman, M., & Rosenman, R. H. (1974). *Type A behavior and your heart.* New York: Faucet Crest.

Friedman, M., Thoresen, C. E., Gill, J. J., Powell, L. H., Ulmer, D., Thompson, L., Price, V. A., Rabin, D. D., Breall, W. S., Dixon, T., Levy, R., & Bourg, E. (1984). Alteration of Type A behavior and reduction in cardiac recurrences in postmyocardial infarction patients. *American Heart Journal, 108*, 237-248.

Friedman, M., & Ulmer, D. (1984). *Treating Type A behavior and your heart.* New York: Knopf.

Fuller, R., Roth, H., & Long, S. (1983). Compliance with disulfiram treatment of alcoholism. *Journal of Chronic Diseases, 36*, 161-170.

Gentry, W. D., & Kobasa, S. C. (1984). Social and psychological resources mediating stress-illness relationships in humans. In W. D. Gentry (Ed.), *Handbook of behavioral medicine.* New York: Guilford.

Gentry, W. D., & Williams, R. B. (1975). *Psychosocial aspects of myocardial infarction and coronary care.* St. Louis: C. V. Mosby.

Glaser, R., Kiecolt-Glaser, J. K., Speicher, C. E., & Holliday, J. E. (1985). Stress, loneliness, and changes in herpesvirus latency. *Journal of Behavioral Medicine, 8*, 249-260.

Glass, D. C. (1977). *Behavior patterns, stress, and coronary disease.* Hillsdale, NJ: Lawrence Erlbaum.

Glik, D. C. (1985, August). *Psychosocial wellness among spiritual healing participants.* Paper presented before the annual meeting of the Society for the Study of Social Problems, Social Psychiatry Section, Washington, DC.

Glock, C., & Stark, R. (1965). *Religion and society in tension*. Chicago: Rand McNally.

Gorsuch, R. L. (1984). Measurement: The boon and bane of investigating religion. *American Psychologist, 39*, 228-236.

Graham, T. W., Kaplan, B. H., Cornoni-Huntley, J. C., James, S. A., Becker, C., Hames, C. P., & Heyden, S. (1978). Frequency of church attendance and blood pressure elevation. *Journal of Behavioral Medicine, 1*, 37-44.

Haynes, R. B., Taylor, D. W., & Sackett, D. L. (1979). *Compliance in health care*. Baltimore: Johns Hopkins University Press.

Hesse, H. (1951) *Siddhartha* (33rd printing). New York: New Directions.

Holmes, A. (1985). *The making of a Christian mind*. Downers Grove, IL: Intervarsity Press.

Hood, R. W. (1975). The construction and preliminary validation of a measure of reported mystical experience. *Journal for the Scientific Study of Religion, 14*, 29-41.

Ingram, R. E. (1987). *Self-focused attention in clinical disorders: Review and a conceptual model*. Paper submitted for publication.

Jacob, R. G., Kraemer, H. C., & Agras, W. S. (1977). Relaxation therapy in the treatment of hypertension: A review. *Archives of General Psychiatry, 34*, 1417-1427.

Jacobson, E. (1939). Variation of blood pressure with skeletal muscle tension and relaxation. *Annals of Internal Medicine, 12*, 1194-1212.

James, W. (1903). *The varieties of religious experience*. New York: Random House.

Jenkins, C. D. (1971). Psychology and social precursors of coronary disease. *New England Journal of Medicine, 284*, 3-23.

Kaplan, B. H. (1976). A note on religious beliefs and coronary disease. *Journal of the South Carolina Medical Association* (Suppl.), 60-64.

Kiecolt-Glaser, J. K. (1986, March). Marital quality, marital disruption and immune function. In M. Jasnoski, *Clinical psychoneuroimmunology in health and disease*. Symposium presented before the Society of Behavioral Medicine, San Francisco.

Kiecolt-Glaser, J. K., Fisher, L. D., Oqrocki, P. et al. (in press). Marital quality, marital disruption, and immune function. *Psychosomatic Medicine*.

Kiecolt-Glaser, J. K., & Glaser, R. (1987). Psychosocial moderators of immune function. *Annals of Behavioral Medicine, 9*, 16-20.

King, M. B., & Hunt, R. A. (1975). Measuring the religious variable: National replication. *Journal for the Scientific Study of Religion, 14*, 13-22.

Kobasa, S. K. (1979). Stressful life events, personality, and health: An inquiry into hardiness. *Journal of Personality and Social Psychology, 37*, 1-11.

Kobasa, S. K., Maddi, S. R., & Kahn, S. (1982). Hardiness and health: A prospective study. *Journal of Personality and Social Psychology, 42*, 168-177.

Krantz, D. S., Grunberg, N. E., & Baum, A. (1985). Health psychology. *Annual Review of Psychology, 36*, 349-383.

Kushner, H. S. (1983). *Why bad things happen to good people*. New York: Avon.

Levy, R. I., & Moskowitz, J. (1982). Cardiovascular research: Decades of progress, a decade of promise. *Science, 217*, 121-129.

Lewis, G. R. (1984). The attributes of God. In W. Elwell (Ed.), *Evangelical dictionary of theology*. Grand Rapids: Baker.

Lewis, K. N., & Lewis, D. A. (1985). Impact of religious affiliation of therapists' judgements of patients. *Journal of Consulting and Clinical Psychology, 53*, 926-932.

Lipid Research Clinics Program. (1984a). The Lipid research clinics coronary primary prevention trial results: I. Reduction in incidence of coronary heart disease. *Journal of the American Medical Association, 251*, 351-364.

Lipid Research Clinics Program. (1984b). The Lipid research clinics coronary primary prevention trial results: II. The relationship of reduction in incidence of coronary heart disease to cholesterol lowering. *Journal of the American Medical Association, 251*, 365-374.

Long, P. J. (1971). The application of psychophysical methods to the study of psychotherapy and behavior modification. In A. E. Bergin & S. L. Garfield (Eds.) *Handbook of Psychotherapy and Behavior Change: An Empirical Analysis*, pp. 75-125. New York: John Wiley.

Martin, J. E., & Dubbert, P. M. (1982). Exercise in behavioral medicine: Current status and future directions. *Journal of Consulting and Clinical Psychology, 50*, 1004-1017.

Martin, J. E., & Dubbert, P. M. (1984). Behavioral management strategies for improving health and fitness. *Journal of Cardiac Rehabilitation, 4*, 200-208.

Martin, J. E., & Dubbert, P. M. (1985). Adherence to exercise. (Vol. Ed., R. L. Terjung). *Exercise and Sport Sciences Reviews, 13*, 137-167.

Maslow, A. H. (1970). *Motivation and personality* (2nd ed.). New York: Harper & Row.

Matarazzo, J. D. (1980). Behavioral health and behavioral medicine: Frontiers for a new health psychology. *American Psychologist, 35*, 807-817.

McClelland, D. (1985, March). [Invited address]. Meeting of the Society of Behavioral Medicine, New Orleans.

McMillen, S. J. (1963). *None of these diseases*. Westwood, NJ: Fleming H. Rebell.

Meadow, M. J. (1984). *Psychology of religion*. New York: Harper & Row.

Medalie, J. H., Kahn, H. A., Neufeld, H. N., Riss, E., & Goldbourt, U. (1973). Five-year myocardial infarction incidence—II. Association of single variables to age and birthplace. *Journal of Chronic Diseases, 26*, 329-349.

Meichenbaum, D., & Jaremko, M. E. (Eds.). (1983). *Stress reduction and prevention*. New York: Plenum.

Mendelsohn, R. (1987, July 7). [Television interview]. Christian Broadcasting Network.

Miller, N. E. (1983). Behavioral medicine: Symbiosis between laboratory and clinic. *Annual Review of Psychology, 34*, 1-31.

Miura, M., & Usa, S. (1970). A psychotherapy of neurosis: Morita therapy. *Psychologia, 13*, 18-35.

O'Brien, O. (1982). Religious faith and adjustment of long-term hemodialysis. *Journal of Religion and Health, 21*, 68-80.

Panush, R. S. (1987). Nutritional therapy for rheumatic diseases. *Annals of Internal Medicine, 106*, 619-621.

Parker, W. R., & St. Johns, E. (1957). *Prayer can change your life: Experiments and techniques in prayer therapy*. Englewood Cliffs, NJ: Prentice-Hall.

Patel, C. (1975). Twelve-month follow-up of yoga and biofeedback in the management of hypertension. *Lancet*, pp. i, 62.

Pizzo, P. A., Robichaud, K. J., Edwards, B. K., Schumaker, C., Kramer, B. S., & Johnson, A. (1983). Oral antibiotic prophylaxis in patients with cancer: A double-blind randomized placebo-controlled trial. *Journal of Pediatrics, 102*, 125-133.

Pooling Project Research Group. (1975). Relationship of blood pressure, serum cholesterol, smoking habit, relative weight and ECG abnormalities to incidence of major coronary events. *Journal of Chronic Diseases, 31*, 201-306.

Powell, L. H., & Thoresen, C. E. (1985). Behavioral and physiologic determinants of long-term prognosis after myocardial infarction. *Journal of Chronic Diseases, 38*, 253-263.

Powell, L. H., & Thoresen, C. E. (1987). Modifying the Type A behavior pattern: A small group treatment approach. In J. A. Blumenthal & D. C. McKee (Eds.), *Applications in behavioral medicine and health psychology: A clinician's source book* (pp. 171-207). Sarasota, FL: Professional Resource Exchange.

Powell, L. H., Thoresen, C. E., Friedman, M. et al. (1986, March). *Clinical techniques to alter the Type A behavior pattern: Part 2—Alteration of the Type A attitudes and beliefs.* Workshop presented before the Society of Behavioral Medicine, San Francisco.

Princeton Religion Research Center. (1986). *Faith development and your ministry.* Princeton, NJ: Author.

Propst, R. (1980). The comparative efficacy of religious and nonreligious imagery for the treatment of mild depression in religious individuals. *Cognitive Therapy and Research, 4,* 167-178.

Prue, D. M., Davis, C. J., Martin, J. E., & Moss, R. A. (1983). An investigation of a minimal contact brand fading program for smoking treatment. *Addictive Behaviors, 8,* 307-310.

Review Panel on Coronary-Prone Behavior and Coronary Heart Disease. (1981). Coronary-prone behavior and coronary heart disease: A critical review. *Circulation, 63,* 1199.

Robinson, J. P., & Shaver, P. R. (1973). *Measures of social psychological attitudes.* Ann Arbor, MI: Institute for Social Research.

Rosenhan, D. (1987, April 2). *What religiosity does for religious people: Some very early findings.* Invited keynote address, Seventh Annual San Diego State University Psychology Enrichment Day, San Diego.

Rosenman, R. H., Friedman, M., Strauss, R., Wurm, M., Kositchek, R., Hahn, W., & Werthessen, N. T. (1984). A predictive study of coronary heart disease: The Western Collaborative Group Study. *Journal of the American Medical Association, 189,* 103.

Sarason, I. G., Sarason, B. R., Potter, E. H., & Antoni, M. H. (1985). Life events, social support, and illness. *Psychosomatic Medicine, 47,* 156-163.

Scherwitz, L., Berton, K., & Leventhal, H. (1978). Type A behavior, self-involvement and cardiovascular response. *Psychosomatic Medicine, 40,* 593-609.

Scherwitz, L., & Canick, J. (1987). Self-reference and coronary heart disease risk. In K. Houston & C. R. Snyder (Eds.), *Type A behavior pattern: Current trends and future directions.* New York: John Wiley.

Scherwitz, L., Granditz, G., Graham, L., Buehler, T., & Billings, J. (1986). Self-involvement and CHD incidence in MRFIT. *Psychosomatic Medicine, 48,* 187-199.

Segal, B. (1986). *Love, medicine and miracles.* New York: Harper & Row.

Thoresen, C. (1987, June). *Development and modification of Type A behavior pattern.* Paper presented at San Diego State University Summer Symposium, "Type A Coronary Prone Behavior Pattern: A Comprehensive Look," San Diego.

Thorensen, C. E., Friedman, M., Powell, L. H., Gill, J. J., & Ulmer, D. (1985). Altering the Type A behavior pattern in post-infarction patients. *Journal of Cardiopulmonary Rehabilitation, 5,* 258-266.

Wallace, R. K., & Benson, H. (1972). The physiology of meditation. *Scientific American, 226*(2). (Reprinted in D. Shapiro et al., (Eds.)., 1972, *Biofeedback & Self-Regulation.* Chicago: Aldine)

Weisz, J. R., Rothbaum, F. M., & Blackburn, T. C. (1984). Standing out and standing in: The psychology of control in America and Japan. *American Psychologist, 39,* 955-969.

Williams, R. B., Jr. (1984). Type A behavior and coronary heart disease: Something old, something new. *Behavioral Medicine Update, 6*, 29-33.

Wolf, S. (1976, February). Protective social forces that counterbalance stress. *Journal of the South Carolina Medical Association*, pp. 57-59.

6

The Relationship Between a Personal Theology and Chronic Pain

ELLIE T. STURGIS

In his book, *The Little Prince*, Saint-Exupery tells the story of a small boy who lives alone on Asteroid B-612 and spends his days enjoying the limited opportunities there. After a time, however, the boy desires wider experiences and flies off to visit other planets. He seeks wisdom by learning about love and life. While visiting earth, he meets a wise fox who teaches him about relationships, risks, and the values of uniqueness. Eventually, when the boy prepares to leave earth, the fox tells him, "It is only through the heart one can see rightly; what is essential is invisible to the eye" (Saint-Exupery, 1943, p. 70).

Behavioral psychologists—as students of the understanding, prediction, and control of observable behavior—largely rejected the philosophy of the fox. That which was not observable and quantifiable was not subjected to scientific scrutiny. Using such an approach, we have learned to help many individuals cope with and manage their anxieties, fears, depressions, and illnesses. Over time, however, we have begun to appreciate the importance of things not directly observable. For instance, as we realized that the cognitions of our clients were important, we began to address the roles that thoughts and attitudes play in disabilities. Even then, as before, we avoided issues such as spirituality and faith, because they were considered unscientific, unquantifiable, and value-laden.

During the past several years, through my work with patients experiencing chronic pain, I have gained an increasing appreciation for the importance of spiritual issues to many clients. Some patients have appeared to be totally defeated by their suffering, while others actually appeared to live more meaningful lives as a result of the experience. After considerable thought, I have come to consider the constructs of spirituality and religiosity to be as valid for empirical examination as the hypothetical construct of anxiety, a topic that has been investigated by behaviorists since the early 1900s (e.g., Jones, 1924).

The spiritual beliefs of an individual are considered important therapeutic issues if they interfere with growth, acceptance, and physical or psychological adaptation; if they interfere with one's ability to deal with stress or set goals; or if they provide effective coping strategies and comfort to patients that improve their ability to adapt. If the religious beliefs are dysfunctional, the therapist may need to assist the patient in the development of more functional beliefs and practices. On the other hand, if the beliefs are adaptive and aid in coping abilities, the therapist may work with the patient concerning ways to enhance his or her use of spirituality in the recovery process. The remainder of this chapter will explore ways in which a person's theological or spiritual beliefs may influence the experience of chronic pain and suffering.

Pain and Suffering

The gate control theory presents a multidimensional model of pain. This theory suggests that pain results from an interaction of physical, cognitive, and emotional factors (Melzack & Wall, 1965). The gate control theory suggests that the transmission of pain signals can be modulated by gating mechanisms located at numerous anatomical levels. The theory proposes that a neural mechanism in the spinal cord acts as a gate that can transmit or inhibit the flow of nerve impulses from peripheral nerve fibers to the central nervous system. When the magnitude of the signal passing through the gate exceeds a critical level, the neural areas responsible for pain experience and response are activated, and the person perceives pain (Turk, Meichenbaum, & Genest, 1983). The amount of pain and discomfort an individual experiences is not only affected by the intensity and type of physical stimulation, however, but is also affected by descending influences from the brain, which are mediated by motivational-affective and cognitive-evaluative processes (Melzack & Dennis, 1978). In other words, suffering is not the inevitable consequence of painful stimulation (Cassel, 1982). One's theological beliefs may affect those descending neural influences and thus directly or indirectly affect the pain experience.

McCandless (1978) has discussed the relationship between pain and suffering and made several conclusions. First, the experience of suffering can be destructive or creative. In destructive suffering, the pain is seen as negative and debilitating; whereas, in creative suffering, the person uses the experience as a stimulus for growth. In the latter, the pain still hurts and is fully experienced, but the ultimate impact of the pain upon the individual is positive. The person apparently uses the experience of mourning and loss as a stimulus to remember the good times of the past, to come to grips with the present, and to use various sources of support to enhance endurance and strength. The process of creative suffering results in growing beyond the pain.

The concepts of destructive and creative suffering are applicable to the types of responses patients often show in response to chronic pain. There are some patients who appear to be conquered or debilitated by their pain. Pain becomes the primary focus of their lives, and most of their experience is filtered through their pain. Others, by contrast, seem to grow through the suffering and continue to live happy and productive lives in spite of their difficulties. The typical predictors of the outcome (type or extent of injury, age, sex, or socioeconomic status) do not discriminate the two groups of pain patients. Reinforcement contingencies and premorbid history are important but are also incomplete predictors of response to pain. In my work with chronic pain patients, it often appears that the spiritual perspective of the patient and the attitude toward his or her role in the world affects the nature of the pain response. In particular, the theme of alienation appears relevant to the ultimate response to pain.

Alienation and Loss

One of the most common complaints I hear from patients who have been seriously injured or have suffered a progressive, debilitating disease is that they experience overwhelming feelings of loss. They no longer enjoy their former state of prowess, health, or freedom to engage actively in life's reinforcers and comforts. Indeed, patients often report feeling alienated as the pain experience becomes chronic. Alienation has been defined as the act of making unfriendly, hostile, or indifferent those relations where attachment, love, and affection once existed. Martin Buber (1970) characterized alienation as the transformation of "I-Thou" relationships into "I-It" relationships. In an I-Thou relationship, the person or object involved in an interaction is viewed as being unique and valuable. In the I-It relationship, the recipient is viewed as a replaceable thing or an object of little or no value. Persons can feel alienated on a number of levels including the physical, personal, interactional, and spiritual. Each type of alienation has different implications for outcome in the experience of chronic pain.

Physical alienation occurs when the person's perception of his or her body no longer matches the self-concept. The perceptions of the body are incongruent with the expectations the individual has for him- or herself. In the case of illness and injury, the body is often viewed as a machine that has broken and is in need of being fixed. The search for the "right" medication, procedure, or surgery is a frequent manifestation of the body-machine concept. In our current society, if an object is no longer reparable, we think of it as valueless, and we usually throw it away and replace it with a new, improved model. We seldom think in terms of patching up and continuing to use the machine in its altered, often diminished form. Even with the technology of twentieth-century medicine, repairs seldom restore the body to its previous level of functioning, and replacement of parts or functions is often impossible. If the body can no longer accomplish the previous functions, it may be seen as an impediment to be overcome or left behind. When the abilities of the physical body limit potential actions, people often begin to generalize their concepts of impairment to their sense of personal growth. This is particularly true in our task-oriented "Me"-generation, which values product over process or things over humanity.

Personal alienation occurs when the sense of self-efficacy is diminished. Many of our ideas of who we are result from what we do or can do. In our task-oriented society, we are typically reinforced by what we accomplish. We are not geared to deal with failure and often do not know how to fail productively (McCandless, 1978). We are hesitant to take responsibility for our actions if the outcome is not a successful one. If our ability to act becomes limited, the sense of self-efficacy can be diminished, and feelings of helplessness and depression increase. With the increased depression, pain may increase, leaving less energy to be expended. Consequently, our performance and efficiency deteriorate, further diminishing feelings of self-worth, and the cycle of further alienation continues.

Interpersonal alienation often follows personal alienation. Loneliness is a frequent result of pain, for the sufferer fails to find anyone who understands or is willing to listen to feelings about the pain experience. The person in pain often needs someone to hear or understand, to help carry the burden of suffering while not reinforcing the exhibition of pain behavior. The process of grieving has been described as involving multiple stages including denial, depression, anger, bargaining, and finally acceptance (Kubler-Ross, 1969). Progression through these stages takes time, and the support of others can be very beneficial in the patient's progression and eventual outcome.

Interpersonal interactions can also influence the ways in which pain is expressed (Fordyce, 1976). If one receives attention only when exhibiting signs of suffering, the likelihood of pain behavior or suffering increases. Conversely, attention given to rehabilitative efforts or healthy behavior is likely to increase the probability of their occurrence. In addition, if the environment ignores pain complaints rather than attending to them, the complaints are likely to escalate to force a termination of the aversive silence. If the escalation results in increased attention, positive or negative, the complaining behavior is negatively reinforced and further complaining is likely. This may then further antagonize those with whom the patient is interacting. Regardless, the nature of the interaction will affect the development of interpersonal alienation.

The alienation can also occur in other ways. As a person becomes more depressed as the result of a disability, he or she is likely to regard him- or herself as inferior to others, and may begin to withdraw from contact with others. As the withdrawal increases, the person has fewer opportunities to be affirmed by others and the sense of self continues to deteriorate. The hurting "independent" person often avoids burdening others with his or her problems, fearing rejection or being labeled as weak (McCandless, 1978). The person in pain also often describes increased difficulties interacting with others because of decreased energy and increased irritability. Comparisons with the abilities of others can also present problems as one experiences feelings of jealousy for another's abilities. "Why me?" is one of the most frequent questions uttered by individuals who are suffering. If one views the self as increasingly deficient, fears of rejection may begin to surface, often resulting in further withdrawal from those who might be a source of support and affirmation. The pain patient can also drive others away by constantly complaining of the pain and reciting his or her difficulties.

As mentioned before, problems in interpersonal alienation may also result from the actions and feelings of others. Those in contact with the patient may begin to have feelings of guilt about their continued health and success, and withdraw from contact with the patient. In addition, certain types of suffering embarrass others, and they hesitate to make contact with the patient because they do not know how to interact comfortably with him or her (McCandless, 1978). Unfortunately, others can increase feelings of alienation by condemning certain emotional or physical problems experienced by the patient. For instance, some may regard the sufferer as faking and just not wanting to work. Others may view the patient as being disabled because of a lack of faith or as punishment for past sins. These, often well-meaning, individuals may try to convince the patient that healing will occur if he or she will only "get right with God" or have enough faith. Unsuccessful healing services can further convince the patient and others around him or her that a moral deficiency underlies the problem. In each of these cases, further interpersonal alienation, destructive to feelings of self-worth and self-efficacy, is likely to occur (McCandless, 1978). Finally, interactional alienation may increase if either of the persons lose respect for the integrity and worth of the other, thus destroying the mutuality of the interaction, a characteristic critical for the maintenance of I-Thou relationships. Any interpersonal interactions resulting in a loss of respect and mutuality contribute to problems of alienation.

Spiritual alienation can also occur during the process of prolonged pain and suffering. During difficult times, people often feel abandoned by God. Our concept of what God is or whether God exists comes through our experiences and learning. Most individuals grow up with the thought that God is omnipotent, that good people deserve good experiences, and that our bad experiences are the result of sin (Kushner, 1981). Bad luck or painful experiences are seen as the result of punishment or as capable of being changed if an omnipotent God would only intervene. If the change does not come, then one feels forsaken by either an uncaring or unjust God, and spiritual alienation results.

As multidimensional alienation can be viewed as a result of injury, illness, or pain, the personal theology of the individual can affect the experience of suffering, the pain experienced by the person, and the subsequent adaptation and rehabilitation of the person. The term *personal theology* is used to describe how a person perceives God as functioning in the world as well as one's sense of purpose in life.

Integrating Faith and Suffering: A Theology of Pain

Faith and suffering can be integrated in three ways. We can be comforted by the faith and retain it; we can maintain our faith while not understanding why events are happening the way they are; or we can give up the faith (Schmitt, 1979). While the book of Job indicates that God lets his children be afflicted by suffering to prove their loyalty, the Christian perspective is different. The New Testament view of suffering as depicted in 1 Peter is that suffering is a means of purifying or ennobling the soul, bringing us into closer fellowship with Christ and leading to a more harmonious life in congruence with God's will.

Suffering can be negative and destructive or can be positive and constructive (McCandless, 1978). Destructive suffering results from one's concept of the nature of God and the way God functions in the world. If one holds a punitive concept of God—one who punishes or ignores one's needs—then efforts of rehabilitation and growth will likely be impeded. First, much of the already diminished energy of the person may be invested in bargaining with God, feeling angry, and feeling depressed and abandoned. Rehabilitation and growth require significant stores of energy, thus time spent in anger and frustration slow the healing process.

Second, if one believes that the pain constitutes punishment for real or imagined "sins," motivation for change can be reduced. Some patients I have seen have considered their condition to be a punishment dealt by God and have considered it sacrilege to try to help themselves. They developed a helpless stance as they waited for God to improve their physical condition once they had paid sufficient penance. If a patient has this perspective, rehabilitation efforts conducted during this period are often unsuccessful, and the individual may actually deteriorate further while waiting for the occurrence of the anticipated healing.

Third, a punitive view of God can influence the sense of self-worth of the individual; after all, the pain is viewed as occurring as a consequence of bad behavior or sins. Some individuals see themselves as undeserving of improvement or rehabilitation; consequently, they do not participate fully in rehabilitative efforts. Again, the concept of a punishing God can reduce the individual's motivation to alter behavior patterns.

A forgiving concept of a loving God, however, can transform the experience of suffering into an experience of growth. This view maintains that we are fundamentally loved, we can destroy or create options through our actions, and we can choose our attitudes and responses toward painful experiences. A forgiving orientation neither eliminates nor necessarily shortens the duration of the pain experience, but it may enable the person to find external resources that will reinforce personal strengths and allow him or her to move forward through the pain. Such responses may actually reduce the impact of the suffering from the pain and can diminish the impact of the commonly occurring alienation.

A positive theology of God stresses the fact that God is forgiving and can be an ever present source of support and strength. God may not be like Superman, rushing in to change the situation, to save the day, and to rescue the weak from threatening or painful situations; but the belief in a higher power can provide a perspective of loving acceptance and comfort. Faith in such a concept can provide the reassurance necessary for one to regard all experience as potentially positive and capable of producing growth. Security comes in the belief that one can cope and overcome difficulties and losses or can learn to live fully with whatever happens (Ihloff, 1976). Bonnell (1969) has described the truly religious person as one who lives by faith in what is and what can be.

This forgiveness model of healing is relevant to the concept of illness-induced alienation, which results from feelings of anger and anxiety about the physical condition. Pattison (1965) defines two models of forgiveness, a punishment and a reconciliation model. The punishment model has a judgmental, bargaining flavor whereby transgressions are punished and improvement results from suffering and learning from one's mistakes. Punishment (and pain) becomes requisite for forgiveness. In the reconciliation model, on the other hand, anxiety and pain are viewed as resulting not from acts or behavior, but from estrangement from sources of love (for body, self, other, or God). The reconciliation model of forgiveness involves the conscious willfulness of the forgiver and forgiven to seek reunion, the reconciliation of the guilty one with the offended one. The I-Thou relationship is the goal of healing. The model proposes that six steps are involved in healing: guilt, confession, remorse, restitution, mutual acceptance, and reconciliation (Pattison,

1965). While the model assumes the actions of individuals influence the development of chronic pain, it does not imply that individuals are solely responsible for the development of pain problems. There are innocent victims of circumstance. What is of issue here is the healing of the alienation that often results from pain. The way in which the model can be used for conceptualizing is described below.

For reconciliation to occur, the individual must first acknowledge his or her guilt or responsibility in the current condition and in the healing process. For example, patients may recognize how their activities or inactivities affect their physical endurance and ability, how their complaining behavior turns others away, or how their anger toward God for letting this happen preoccupies their thinking. This recognition is only a first step in the healing process. Some patients stop at this phase and become stuck, blaming themselves and rejecting opportunities to grow beyond their current condition. Thus, recognition, a form of insight, is necessary but not sufficient for rehabilitation.

Once the person has acknowledged his or her role in the alienation, a sense of remorse typically occurs. Remorse is not restricted to regret. It is the recognition of the alienation-generated hostility and the desire to be reconciled with that which has been rejected. True remorse is not self-condemnation used as a way to elicit sympathy nor is it a wallowing in self-pity. Remorse is a motivating source that spurs the person to begin the process of putting life back together and involves learning to live as full a life as possible despite the existing conditions and limitations.

In the restitution phase, the punitive and forgiveness models are most distinct. In a punitive model of forgiveness, restitution constitutes an effort to avoid retaliation. In the reconciliation model, restitution establishes the I-Thou condition. Restoration occurs as a function of loving, of accepting again, the alienated entity. The body, injured and disabled as it is, is accepted as worthy of rehabilitation. The person accepts that he or she is worthy of a better life and better relations, of continued growth and development, and of recovery and rehabilitation.

In the acceptance phase, the fifth phase of the forgiveness process, unqualified love becomes important. In acceptance, the forgiven must share the guilt, anguish, and estrangement of the alienated. In true acceptance, the mutual separation is experienced and the forgiver extends his or her love to the estranged, accepting as worthy that which has been alienated. This may involve acceptance of all levels previously experienced as being alienated: physical, personal, interpersonal, and spiritual. Mutual acceptance does not ignore the magnitude of the estrangement, seek payment for punishment, nor use the opportunity as an occasion to justify or advance the self. It is a reunion of estranged, separated, and rejected parts of a whole (Pattison, 1965). If I-Thou relationships are to be restored, the patient must accept the body, self, and relationships as being of worth and rehabilitatable. The acceptance may involve forgiveness of the self for past actions, understanding that the past cannot be undone nor restored. Energy begins to be invested in the future where change can occur. Acceptance may also involve forgiveness for the inability to be omnipotent; the person accepts the existing limitations. The creative question becomes, "Now that this has happened or these conditions exist, what do I do to maximize meaning in my life? Where do I go from here? How do I invest my energies and abilities?" This marks the true beginning of a constructive orientation to rehabilitation.

Reconciliation, the final phase of forgiveness, occurs as the individual once again begins to trust his or her abilities. Reconciliation is the completed restoration of the I-Thou relationship, a concept of wholeness and of infinite potential. It is the restoration of feelings of respect and love, the ultimate expression of healing.

Case Study

The importance of considering spiritual as well as physical and psychological perspectives in rehabilitation may be seen in the discussion of Mr. K., a 40-year-old male referred to a chronic pain center for treatment of pain of three years duration secondary to a work-related accident. The patient had sustained an injury at the L-5, S-1 level of the spinal cord resulting in chronic back and right leg pain, problems with elimination and urinary incontinence, and sexual impotence. He had undergone three surgical procedures as a result of the injury including microsurgery of the facet joints, a laminectomy, and a spinal fusion. Pain complaints continued and, at the time of referral, the patient was taking up to 15 Percodan tablets per day, drank whiskey episodically, and also took other pain medications as he could obtain them. He visited the local emergency room about three times per month for shots of Demerol. He was described by his wife as being "out of it" much of the time, being very irritable, and spending most of the day in the reclining chair watching television and sleeping.

Prior to the accident, he had been a very hard worker, an attentive husband, a deacon in the church, and the male soloist in the choir; had coached a church softball team; and had been a very gregarious individual. He presented with problems of pain; depressed mood with difficulties of sleep onset, nocturnal and early morning awakenings, increased weight, suicidal ideation, and difficulty concentrating. He also demonstrated irritability and talked about his pain much of the time.

The patient was withdrawn from the narcotic medications and placed on a trial of antidepressant medications with no untoward side effects. An aggressive physical therapy regimen was developed to teach him to relax musculature diagnosed as being involved in the pain, to pace his activities more appropriately, to perform activities safely, and to restore him to as healthy a condition as possible. Psychological counseling targeted his self-deprecating thinking and taught him alternative methods to relax and control the pain. He repeatedly returned to thoughts of questioning why the injury had happened to him, and he insisted on repeatedly searching his past for transgressions that might have led to his injury and condition. The wife was involved in the therapeutic process, learning to support more healthy moves on his part and working on improving communication skills. While the patient participated in therapy, he made minimal gains. Serum levels indicated the antidepressant dosage was within the therapeutic range, but no real change in mood was observed. The patient did, however, begin sleeping better. Several times during the hospitalization, I attempted to broach the subject of his feelings of guilt and to question how he could view his life as being productive if he could not prove his worth through being so actively involved in all aspects of living. He consistently refused to deal with these issues, and was eventually discharged from the hospital free of the medication problem, but largely unchanged in other dimensions of his life. During the next few months, the patient showed a difficult recovery. He remained drug-free but continued to be very despondent, angry, and helpless. Referral to another treatment center was considered but he was not interested, feeling that his condition was his lot in life.

About nine months following discharge from the hospital, he called and scheduled an appointment. At this time, his affect was much brighter, he acknowledged the pain, but he reported a slow increase in activities with the family and with the church and that he had become involved in a correspondence course. Questioning revealed that a change had occurred about three months earlier when he began spending some time with another patient previously treated at the clinic who was also a member of his church. This person spent much time with him talking about the importance of deciding what he was to do with the "broken, but repaired vessel" in which he lived. The patient worked with him to accept his condition as one that might be improved but not miraculously changed. They spent some time together with the minister who allowed him to express anger to God and began to focus upon his plans for the future. When he began to reach out to others, they responded in a supportive fashion. When he pushed himself too hard and became too involved in activities at the church and home, others helped him to slow down and reminded him that actions were less important than faith and a willing attitude.

The changes in the clinical presentation were remarkable, and with the changes in the patient's perspective, he increased his use of techniques and procedures learned at the pain clinic. Now, two years post-treatment, the patient is employed at a sedentary job, is again involved with family and the church, continues to have pain, but lives within the limits of the pain. His primary function in the church has become one of visiting those in distress. In this case, I believe that, until spiritual issues were addressed by an individual whom he trusted and knew to be of good faith, the rehabilitation efforts were of minimal utility.

Summary

The healing process described as fundamental to rehabilitation involves time and the adoption of a perspective different from our twentieth-century mentality. Our society is geared toward success, comfort, speed, and efficiency. Disability or suffering represent challenges to these ideals. We are not used to settling for repair, pain, gradual recovery, and partial restoration of functioning. Alienation or feelings of loneliness and separateness are uncomfortable and can actually interfere with the process of healing and rehabilitation. As therapists working with individuals with chronic pain problems, we are faced with varied problems that are affected by type of injury and disability, type of deterioration, the reinforcement history, cognitive and emotional abilities, and so on. All of these factors affect the rehabilitation of the patient. In addition to these variables, however, many patients have concepts of God and of forgiveness that can interfere with or assist in the rehabilitation process. If the theological concepts of the patients interfere with healing, these need to be considered. Effective therapy will consider the total person and attempt to help the patient accept him- or herself as worthy of the efforts of rehabilitation. We have developed valuable rehabilitation procedures designed to increase health and decrease illness behavior. As responsible professionals, let us make sure we are broad-minded in our approaches and consider all essential aspects of our patients—the biological, emotional, and spiritual—as we plan our rehabilitation programs and assist clients in their journeys to health.

REFERENCES

Bonnell, G. C. (1969). Salvation and psychotherapy. *Journal of Religion and Health, 8,* 382-398.

Buber, M. (1970). *I and thou.* New York: Scribner.

Cassel, E. J. (1982). The nature of suffering and the goals of medicine. *New England Journal of Medicine, 306,* 639-645.

Fordyce, W. E. (1967). *Behavioral methods for chronic pain and illness.* St. Louis: C. V. Mosby.

Ilhoff, R. W. (1976). Suffering to grow. *Journal of Religion and Health, 15,* 164-180.

Jones, M. C. (1924). A laboratory study of fear. The case of Peter. *Pedagogical Seminary, 31,* 308-315.

Kubler-Ross, E. (1969). *On death and dying.* New York: Macmillan.

McCandless, J. B. (1978). Dealing creatively with suffering: The living death. *Journal of Religion and Health, 17,* 19-30.

Melzack, R., & Dennis, S. G. (1978). Neurophysiological foundations of pain. In R. A. Sternbach (Ed.), *The psychology of pain.* New York: Raven.

Melzack, R., & Wall, P. (1965). Pain mechanisms. A new theory. *Science, 50,* 971-979.

Pattison, E. M. (1965). On the failure to forgive or to be forgiven. *American Journal of Psychotherapy, 19,* 106-115.

Saint-Exupery, A. de (1943). *The little prince.* New York: Harcourt, Brace, & World.

Schmitt, R. (1979). Suffering and faith. *Journal of Religion and Health, 18,* 263-275.

Turk, D. C., Meichenbaum, D., & Genest, M. (1983). *Pain and behavioral medicine: A cognitive-behavioral perspective.* New York: Guilford.

7

Gaining Control by Giving Up Control

Strategies for Coping with Powerlessness

JAMES R. BAUGH

If I had to come up with a single word to describe my work as a psychologist, it would be training clients to *control* various aspects of their lives. A tape-set that I produced is titled "Controlling Your Life." I know that feeling "out of control" is one of the most frightening experiences suffered by human beings. I have often taught that controlling one's thoughts will control emotions, which in turn will affect behavior, as does controlling the consequences of that behavior. These are the basic tenets of behavioral psychology and are well documented by volumes of data. Yet I know that, in the reality of life, one of the important controls is to *give up control* in impossible situations. A more accurate statement is that a sense of control can be gained by giving up a desired control that is beyond one's power or ability.

The Paradox of Control

It sounds like double-talk to speak of strength through accepting powerlessness, or of controlling certain aspects of one's life by giving up control. These apparent contradictions, however, are actually potential strategies for healing of some of life's most discouraging experiences—losing something of value and being without hope of escaping the loss or of bringing about a sense of justice or restitution. The loss is complete, the individual gets nothing in return—zero.

People's lives are full of "complete losses." The accompanying sense of powerlessness is one of the most painful emotions experienced. In the extreme, individuals may murder, go "crazy," or kill themselves in an attempt to escape the state of being powerless in situations that they hold dear. People who are powerless to take care of their own needs may become desperate and join the most dangerous elements of society. The state of being powerless is only significant when there is an inability to control situations involved in a loss that is important to the loser.

Much in our lives is under our control. We can avoid some potential difficulties and solve some of the problems that arise (Mahoney, 1979). We can learn to control our feelings, thoughts, and behavior. Our attitudes and basic beliefs are changeable (Lazarus, 1977). We can be trained to control involuntary processes such as writer's cramp (Sanavio, 1982), erectile impotence (Davis & Davis, 1980), and even hiccuping (vanHeuven & Smeets, 1981). Other aspects of our lives are beyond control. We can't control change, stop our bodies and minds from aging, or get others to "do it our way." Niebuhr (Beck, 1980, p. 823), in his 1943 *Serenity Prayer*, advises us of the wisdom to know the difference between those things that can be changed and those things that cannot. There is no power or strength in beating a "dead horse." There is strength in accepting powerlessness when it is true.

Why Should an Individual Ever Give Up?

So what if a person is powerless? If he or she gives up, there is no chance, right? Why not keep trying forever?

When not giving up means not accepting reality, psychopathology may result—the person can become a *chronic victim*. Glasser (1984, p. xiii) in his book on control, mentions an attempt to console a friend following an unexpected marital breakup: "It is clear to everyone but the friend that she is choosing to remain hostage to a marriage that is over."

In 1980, I was a guest on a radio talk show, arranged by my publisher, to market a recently published book. Listeners would call in questions relating to the problem-solving theme of the book. Near the end of the show, an individual called, stating that he was "blind and lived alone." He indicated that his problem had no solution. He related the problems of a blind person living by himself and added that he was sure I could not suggest anything that would give him any relief. What got my attention was the response of the audience who telephoned in answer to the blind man. There was a woman with an inoperable brain tumor, a paraplegic veteran, a second blind person, and others. Their messages were similar, that the blind man need not spend his time suffering but he should *accept his fate and make the best of life.* These callers had accepted their misfortunes and, in most cases, reported gaining strength of character through a serious loss over which they were powerless. I became interested in how these victims of crises had been emotionally healed rather than becoming chronic victims.

I have observed many clinical populations including rape victims, victims of natural disasters, victims of economic disasters, victims of chronic illnesses, addicted persons, people who have been treated unfairly, victims of divorce, and those suffering from post-traumatic syndrome. I have worked extensively with farmers and their families who lost, or were about to lose, the family farm (Neill & Baugh, 1987). People tend to react to these losses much as they do to death of a loved one or knowledge of their own death. Various writers describe this reaction in different ways. Kubler-Ross (1969), whose work has been so widely quoted, suggested that loss is dealt with in stages of denial, anger, bargaining, depression, and acceptance. Other authors mention impact, recoil, and recovery (as in Paykel, 1982; Silverman, 1966); numbness, depression, and recovery (as in Paykel, 1982; Clayton, 1973); disengagement, disidentification, disenchantment, and disorientation (Bridges, 1980); shock, disorganization, volatile emotions, guilt, loss and loneliness, relief, and reestablishment (Kavanaugh, 1974); numbness, yearning, despair, and reorganization (Parkes, 1970).

The descriptions vary, but most of the writers agree that there is an attempt to escape (denial, shock, numbness, and so on), that somewhere in the process there is a deep feeling of gloom (depression, despair, and so on), and that the process ends in acceptance and a return to normal functioning.

This last stage—acceptance—appears to be of utmost importance in putting life's tragedies behind. My observations have been that, following the initial shock of a loss (a small loss or a significant loss), individuals in time either accept that they are powerless, enter into deep sadness, and end by accepting the loss, or they continue to deny the loss. Along with denial, there is a resentment (anger carried over an extended period of time) and magical thinking. This latter reaction can continue for long periods of time and prevents *letting go of the loss*.

The denial is supported by anger, which motivates one to continue solving the problem, and magical thinking, which is based on a belief, "If I stay mad long enough or suffer enough, I will eventually get justice or restitution." This magical thinking is difficult to comprehend and is best demonstrated by the comment of a former client.

The client was referred by his physician for stress-related gastrointestinal problems. During the interview, he revealed a long-standing resentment (which had lasted 22 years) and he admitted to "festering" about it regularly. He agreed to give up the resentment as a part of his stress management. When that aspect of his treatment was broached, however, he responded, "I can't let that S.O.B. off the hook." He *magically* believed his resentment would eventually bring him justice.

Farmers in financial crisis refusing to accept their losses have been observed to express strong resentment. Some seem to get into a cycle of expressing their resentment in anger, blame, or suffering. They look for ways to continue to escape the pain of their losses—for example, denial of the losses, or an increase in alcohol consumption. Any relief through these maneuvers is temporary and the feeling of powerlessness returns. The feeling of powerlessness may be overridden by renewed resentment, which leads to, in turn, the maneuvers above. This cycle may continue for many years, recurring when some remainder of the loss occurs.

It is important to *give up* when the situation is hopeless. The alternative is to continue to battle an impossible foe and endure the stress of an ineffective struggle.

Why Is It So Difficult to Accept the Powerlessness and the Reality of Loss?

To accept that one is powerless, in many, is akin to *giving up hope*. Yet, hope is almost sacred. It is a subject of song, poetry, and the pulpit: "Keep your hopes up"; "All you really need is hope"; "Major virtues are faith, hope and charity." To accept defeat is a show of weakness and, therefore, a threat to pride; whereas continued anger, threatened revenge, or a vow to keep trying are revered. To give up hope seems sacrilegious.

One major stumbling block to acceptance is pride. Pride is a multifaceted perception of self, partly based on skills in mastering the environment (the ability to get things done well, and social skills) and partly based on illusions of being "better than," which includes covering up weaknesses. The more an individual depends on pride as a major source of self-worth, the more difficult it is to admit to a weakness. Facing one's powerlessness in a situation that *counts* is a definite weakness.

Acceptance usually involves the deep feeling of sadness, one of life's most distressing pains. Fighting off acceptance with resentment, denial, and magical thinking feels stronger and much less painful, in the short run anyway. Anger is a major source of strength. Aaron Beck et al. (1979) suggest using induced anger as a therapeutic technique for relieving sadness. Anger feels strong, readies the person to overcome problems involved in the loss, and is preferable to the experience of acceptance and sadness. So, even though moving through the process of grief is *natural*, following a loss, there are *natural* cultural expectations that work against the process.

The Method of Surrender:
A Spiritual Approach

The relationship between accepting powerlessness, surrender, and spirituality (a belief in a power greater than ourselves that can affect our lives) is revealed in the first three steps of Alcoholics Anonymous. As a psychologist working part-time in an alcohol treatment center, "turning one's will over to God" was a hard concept for me to accept. I did not object to religion, as I regularly attended church, but I separated psychology and religion. As with oil and water, I thought that both exist separately and cannot be mixed.

At the treatment center, I observed two general types of attitudes held by different patients. One group accepted what they were being taught, that they were powerless over alcohol, that their lives had become unmanageable, that there was a Power greater than themselves, and that they needed to turn their lives and wills over to this Power or God. They were taught, and accepted, that their willpower was inadequate to change their drinking behavior.

A second group admitted that their lives had become unmanageable but didn't buy the powerless part. They viewed their problem as using poor judgment in drinking and were determined, through willpower, to control their drinking. I identified with this group. After all, I was in the business of training people who were out of control to regain control over their behavior. This second group talked of elaborate plans to strengthen their willpower by going into bars or keeping liquor in their homes and controlling their urges to drink. As time passed, it seemed to me that members of my group failed to stay sober and more often returned for treatment than the other group who surrendered their will.

What does *surrender* mean in psychological and behavioral terms? To surrender our wills to God means to behave as we believe God would want us to behave and to accept whatever happens as a result. In surrendering, one is better able to bear the emotional pain of facing the loss. A strong faith is not absolutely necessary in surrendering. If this were true, very few would find it useful. Most people have doubts. What is important is the discipline to follow the procedure.

Surrender is often useful when the "loss" is control over a compulsion. Brenner (1985, p. 103) states:

> When we give up self-control, we are still fighting an impulse or action; we've simply lost the battle. We might try to avoid this "loss" by fighting harder the next time around. If we count to ten one day and still lose our temper, the next time we get mad we may count to twenty. Struggle, conflict, and resistance predominate. Surrender creates a completely different sensation. Through it we find the joy of diving headlong into an experience. It lets us see what happens when we allow the forces already in place to play themselves out. Surrender generates none of the frustration involved with losing control. It is beginning afresh.

Humility

Surrendering implies that something is greater than oneself. In the alcoholic community, the term used is "Higher Power"—to most this means God. Those with faith in something else, however, may use their AA group as a "higher power" (a collective power greater than themselves). In any case, the implication is one of dependency on something outside of the self. This is a threat to an individual's pride.

According to Jabay, many people have unspoken ideas of omnipotence. These individuals may assume God's attributes. As Jabay (1969, p. 62) puts it, "We insult God by vesting ourselves with His attributes. We take His holy garments, so to speak, and put them on ourselves. Then we play god." Jabay goes on to quote Eric Berne:

> "Everyone believes in the immortality of his being, the irresistibility of his charms, and the omnipotence of his thoughts and feelings" (Berne, p. 27). When Dr. Berne refers to our universal belief in the immortality of our being, he means that we are so self-oriented that our minds will not tolerate the thought that once we were not, and that someday we will not be. (Jabay, 1969, p. 38)

Humility is necessary for true surrender. As the above statements indicate, humility is not easy for any of us. The state of humility is sometimes misunderstood. This concept does not communicate a lower social or moral self. Humility includes knowing your own limitation, honest self-evaluation, accepting your weaknesses, feeling no better than and no less than any other human being, and submission to God. This concept allows one to meet others emotionally eyeball to eyeball and to surrender to God. Buechner (1973, p. 40) says of humility:

> True humility doesn't consist of thinking ill of yourself but of not thinking of yourself much differently from the way you'd be apt to think of anybody else. It is the capacity for being no more and no less pleased when you play your own hand well than when your opponents do.

Self-Surrender

Surrender necessitates giving up self-centeredness and self-glorification and submitting to the will of God or to the higher power of the group. One of the most frequently asked questions in an out-patient addictions program that the author directs is "I'm ready to surrender now, how do I do it?" It is difficult to answer this question in a way that will be helpful to a particular individual. There are, however, many possible answers. For example, a person might image two desks in front of him or her at the beginning of each day. One is the person's own desk and the other is labeled "the Lord's desk." On the first desk are piles of tasks and responsibilities. The person looks over all the duties and decides which ones he or she is capable of handling. The remainder, the ones over which he or she is powerless, are moved over to the Lord's

TABLE 7.1
Manageable and Unmanageable
Behaviors of a Compulsive Overeater

Manageable	Unmanageable
Keep records	Degree of hunger
Daily food plan	Amount eaten (binges)

Monitor
    speed of eating
    size of bites
    food passed up
    degree of hunger
	Snacks in the house
	
	Eating in a restaurant
	
	Eating sweets

Exercise	Hiding food from family
Turn over unmanageable urges to my Higher Power	

desk. The person who shared this particular technique (which he had used regularly for several years) stated that he had to practice "accepting what the Lord did" with the items he transferred. He maintained that this ability increased with practice.

Manageability

The above procedure is an attempt to follow the *Serenity Prayer* by distinguishing those things that can be controlled from those things that cannot, and to accept the results. A similar, but more clinically oriented, technique is to separate behaviors related to a *particular problem* into "manageable" and "unmanageable." Table 7.1 is an example from a compulsive overeater. These two procedures are different from the more frequently used "prayer and meditation." These techniques are mentioned here because some individuals seem to need more concrete procedures. They reject prayer or get discouraged when it doesn't seem to work for them.

Focusing on controlling the "manageable" and "turning over to your Higher Power" those unmanageable factors gets the client away from "willpower" that has a probability of failure (Mahoney, 1979)—away from an internal struggle. For example, if an individual has an urge to eat that piece of cheesecake in the refrigerator, and depends on willpower, he or she will picture the cheesecake in the mind's eye, override the urge to move toward the cheesecake, and feel tension of an internal struggle. The picture usually returns, continuing the struggle. Turning the urge over to God and submitting to God's will relieves the struggle—and, therefore, is a control by giving up control.

Case History:
Resentment Exchanged for Grief

Marion had felt "dirty" and like a bad person since childhood. She was addicted to drugs and had already lived a hard life in her 31 years. She was bright and didn't appreciate it, pretty but didn't feel pretty, and talented as a musician—this last fact the only sense of personal worth that she would accept.

She seemed to be successfully working in her treatment program, except that she would not give up the low opinion of herself—a risk for relapse if not corrected. While working on her fourth step (a moral inventory of her life), she painfully faced sexual abuse by her grandfather, beginning when she was 8 years old. She shared this information with her counselor, adding that she *could not accept* what had happened to her. She felt as responsible as her grandfather for the sexual encounter and hated herself as well as him for it. She was attempting to right the wrong by holding on to resentment toward herself and her grandfather.

If Marion is to move from operations designed to bring about justice, to punish for the deed, toward accepting the misfortune, she must (a) accept that she is powerless to correct what has already happened, (b) be willing to give up her resentment, and (c) grieve (feel sad) over her losses.

To accept powerlessness is to accept hopelessness. Rationally, this should be easy—the past is over and cannot be changed. As mentioned earlier, however, magical thinking and cultural beliefs make acceptance and a willingness to give up resentment difficult. Marion was rationally confronted until she began to understand her original point of view as irrational.

A method used to get Marion into the process of feeling sadness over her losses was to first get her to make a list of those losses. Table 7.2 is a listing of her losses from the sexual abuse.

Marion stated that she never remembered any crying or sadness

TABLE 7.2
Losses from Sexual Abuse

I lost my:

Virginity
Self-worth
Faith in my mother
Trust in men
Right to discover sex normally
Normal sex life
Grandfather
Self-respect
Ideals about marriage
Right to deserve anything
Normal attitude toward men
Ability to feel normal
Ability to get close to anyone
Honesty

---

about the incident, only anger and bitterness. Marion was taught to separate her losses from their cause. It was the cause, the sexual abuse, that maintained her anger. When she put aside this image and thought of her losses, one at a time, she could begin to feel her sadness. She was instructed to think of the losses listed each day, until she could think of them without any discomfort.

There is some disagreement in the literature as to the importance of emotion in completing the grief process. Worden, and most other grief counselors, suggest crying openly as a healthy part of the grieving process. If the crying does not occur spontaneously, Worden (1982, p. 43) states, "There are some occasions when sadness and crying need to be encouraged by the counselor." Clayton (1973) concluded that minimal expression of emotion should be considered a normal style of grieving. She even seemed to be discouraging expressing emotion. Clayton quoted a study by Parkes (1970) suggesting that those most emotional following a death were also the most disturbed one year later. Not all researchers are in agreement, however. *The Harvard Medical School Mental Health Letter* reported a study in which half of the experimental group were exposed to painful memories of the death of a spouse and the other half were asked to avoid thinking of the dead person. The two groups were followed for 20 weeks and the group confronted with the painful memories were better adjusted socially (Grinspoon, 1987). So, some say "cry" and others caution "but not too much." Finding those overly emotional individuals the most disturbed after one year may be explained by the observation that emotion that includes bitterness, self-pity, and a sense of "it's not fair" may continue for a long period of time. These individuals can be long-suffering. Emotional pain with acceptance of the loss and without the anger was short lived (Neill & Baugh, 1987). This latter reaction along with some feeling of emotional pain seems necessary for successful grieving.

Marion's most emotional moment came when she faced the loss of her grandfather, whom she loved. At the moment of sexual contact, he became her seducer, whom she hated. A one-year follow-up revealed Marion had maintained her forgiveness for both her grandfather and herself. She also was relieved of the resentment toward her mother, whom she told of the abuse and who responded, "Please don't tell anyone else."

Case History:
A Wife of An Alcoholic

Sherry had been struggling to "cure" her husband's alcoholism for many years. At first she believed her love would heal his addiction. Later she changed to shaming him, then to withdrawal of love, and finally to threats of a divorce. Of course, he only increased his drinking as a response to the pressure.

Finally she became depressed herself and sought counseling. Previously she had attended a few Al-Anon meetings (for families of alcoholics) and heard the expression "detaching" from the alcoholic family member.

> Family members and friends do not have the power to change alcoholic behavior. No one can control the actions of others, alcoholic or not.

> If friends and relatives will let go of their own often misguided desire to help and allow a spiritual source to guide the alcoholic instead, surprising results often follow. At Al-Anon meeting, members will proudly share how they refrained from making excuses, or covering up the consequences of the drinking, only to find that the alcoholic has taken on some responsibility for himself or herself by paying bills or getting to work.

TABLE 7.3
Manageable and Unmanageable Behaviors of a Wife of an Alcoholic

Manageable	Unmanageable
Stop rescuing	Control John's drinking behavior
Stop complaining about his drinking	
	Feeling angry about John's drinking behavior
Stop looking for and throwing away his hidden bottles	
Pray for help—turn over the unmanageable to God	

> Even if *Let Go and Let God* results in the alcoholic's getting into more trouble—with the law, for instance, or with the boss—the person deeply affected by the drinking comes to realize that he or she is not responsible. (Al-Anon Family Group, 1985, pp. 248-249)

She felt support and understanding from her Al-Anon experience but could never detach for very long. She knew there was a key to John's drinking and she was determined to find it. In counseling, she was encouraged to return to Al-Anon for support and was coached into organizing her experience with her husband into *manageable* and *unmanageable* categories. Table 7.3 is the result of her efforts.

Sherry agreed to pray for God's help but to take no other action in terms of personally controlling John's drinking behavior. She agreed, however, to stop rescuing him from the consequences of his behavior. She would no longer make excuses to his boss (she had a realistic fear of the possibility that he might be terminated). She would no longer comfort him in recovering from his hangover. She would allow the children to have a normal day instead of "Daddy's sick, so be quiet." This was particularly rough on John during the weekend.

She arranged with her brother, her best friend, and her mother to spend the night at one of their houses when John showed signs of intoxication. He always drank in secret. He kept his alcohol in his workshop. John escalated in his alcoholism. He no longer drank in secret. Four months later, John's boss confronted him. He was sent to the personnel department of his company where he was given the option of treatment or facing termination, and chose to enter the treatment program. Whether or not his wife's behavior had anything to do with John's confrontation by his employer is not clear. Her stress level, however, was much relieved by her *giving up control that she didn't have anyway*.

Is it possible to accept a loss too soon? How do you know when it is time to consider the situation a loss rather than a problem to solve? The answer to the first question is "yes." Particularly those individuals who have recently discovered the relief of accepting powerlessness—a relief from the struggle to change the impossible—are likely to accept too soon. These novices begin to accept more and more of their lives as situations over which they are powerless. They get relief through an escape from normal responsibility. They claim powerlessness over situations that they could control with some effort. As to the second question, it is time to consider accepting the state of being powerless when the individual has attempted all of the problem-solving maneuvers that he or she can think of and can come up with no new solutions. It is better to err on the side of trying too long than to give up too soon. To hang on to the illusion of a solution when nothing new is in one's mind, however, is to hang on to the misery of denying reality and continued failure. Even if the problem is solvable but beyond a particular individual's skills, it is time to give up.

Summary

Control of behavior, emotion, environment, consequences, and anything else that is involved in the psychopathology of the individual is the business of behavior therapy. A paradoxical control is to give up the desire and operations to gain control when one is powerless—*control by giving up control*. As the *Serenity Prayer* suggests, it is important to recognize the difference between controllable and uncontrollable factors. To continue to "try to do the impossible" is sometimes seen as admirable in our culture but it is not very smart, particularly for the clinical population with little energy to spare. Two possible avenues to "giving up control" are explored—the grief process and the spiritual approach. The techniques themselves are not the main point; accepting the reality, when powerless to overcome some aspect of one's condition, is the principal concept. Giving up control is difficult. It seems unnatural and undesirable. The cultural and personal blocks to giving up control are explored.

REFERENCES

Al-Anon Family Group. (1985). *Al-anon faces alcoholism.* New York: Al-Anon Family Group Headquarters.

Beck, A. T., Rush, A. J., & Shaw, B. F. (1979). *Cognitive therapy of depression.* New York: Guilford.

Beck, E. M. (1980). *Familiar quotations* (15th ed.). Boston: Little, Brown.

Berne, E. (1957). *A layman's guide to psychiatry and psychoanalysis.* New York: Simon & Schuster.

Brenner, E. (1985). *Winning by letting go: Control without compulsion, surrender without defeat.* New York: Harcourt Brace Jovanovich.

Bridges, W. (1980). *Transitions.* Philippines: Addison-Wesley.

Buechner, F. (1973). *Wishful thinking: A theological ABC.* New York: Harper & Row.

Clayton, P. J. (1973). The period of numbness. *The Director,* pp. 4-5.

Clayton, P. J. (1982). Bereavement. In E. S. Paykel (Ed.), *Handbook of affective disorders* (chap. 30). New York: Guilford.

Davis, R., & Davis, T. (1980). Treatment of erectile impotence using a nocturnal tumescence conditioning procedure. *Journal of Behavior Therapy and Experimental Psychiatry, 11*(1), 63-66.

Glasser, W. (1984). *Take effective control of your life.* New York: Harper & Row.

Grinspoon, L. (1987). Bereavement and grief. *Harvard Medical School Mental Health Letter, 3*(10), 3.

Jabay, E. (1969). *The god-players.* Grand Rapids, MI: Zondervan.

Kavanaugh, R. (1974). *Facing death.* Baltimore: Penguin.

Kubler-Ross, E. (1969). *On death and dying.* New York: Macmillan.

Lazarus, A. (1977). *In the mind's eye.* New York: Rawson Associates.

Mahoney, M. J. (1979). *Self-change: Strategies for solving personal problems.* New York: Norton.

Neill, R. H., & Baugh, J. R. (1987). *How to lose your farm in ten easy lessons—and cope with it.* Leland, MS: Mississippi River.

Parkes, C. M. (1970). The first year of bereavement: A longitudinal study of the reaction of London widows to the deaths of their husbands. *Psychiatry, 33,* 444-467.

Paykel, E. S. (Ed.). (1982). *Handbook of affective disorders.* New York: Guilford.

Sanavio, E. (1982). An operant approach to the treatment of writer's cramp. *Journal of Behavior Therapy and Experimental Psychiatry, 13*(1) 69-72.

Silverman, P. R. (1966). *Services for the widowed during the period of bereavement, social work practice.* New York: Columbia University Press.

Stampfl, T. G., & Levis, D. J. (1967). Essentials of implosive therapy: A learning theory based psychodynamic behavioral therapy. *Journal of Abnormal Psychology, 72,* 496-503.

vanHeuven, P. F., & Smeets, P. M. (1981). Behavioral control of chronic hiccupping associated with gastrointestinal bleeding in a retarded epileptic male. *Journal of Behavior Therapy and Experimental Psychiatry, 12*(4), 341-346.

Worden, J. W. (1982). *Grief counseling and grief therapy: A handbook for the mental health practitioner.* New York: Springer.

8

A Religious Critique of Behavior Therapy

STANTON L. JONES

"What do the data say?" So goes the most frequent question exchanged by behavior therapists when they disagree. Religious beliefs, in behavioral circles, are often seen as the antithesis of data, and so the concept of a religious critique of the assumptions underlying the practice of behavior therapy would seem ludicrous to many behavior therapists. The purposes of this chapter are to establish briefly the propriety of such a religious critique and then to conduct the religious critique from the vantage point of my own particular religious commitments, those of an evangelical Christian. A similar analysis could be conducted from other faith traditions, as the manner in which the critique is conducted is generally applicable. The particular conclusions drawn here are specific to the religious vantage point from which the critique is conducted.

This critique will attempt to explore both points of tension and of compatibility between a particular religious faith commitment and a behavioral view of the person. While the following will at times accentuate the points of tension, it is nevertheless a "friendly" critique. I am both an academician who teaches and conducts research from the

AUTHOR'S NOTE: I wish to express my deepest thanks to my colleagues at Wheaton, Charles R. Carlson, Robert C. Roberts, and W. Jay Wood, who gave graciously of their time and energy in critiquing an earlier draft of this chapter. The deficiencies that remain are my own. I welcome correspondence around the issues raised in this chapter.

cognitive-behavioral perspective and a clinician whose practice has been most directly shaped by the field of behavior therapy over other available personality theories within psychology. There are, however, real tensions between religious and behavioral views of the person that must be addressed.

The conduct of such a religious critique, I believe, is important for every behavior therapist, so that his or her embracing of behavior therapy as a working model will be as compatible as possible with his or her own religious commitments (whether they be traditionally religious or not). Such a critique is important as well for the pastor or religious counselor who wishes to draw intelligently from behavioral methods to enrich his or her counseling practice, because clear knowledge of the undergirding assumptions of behavior therapy will deepen that person's understanding of the field. Finally, a religious critique is important for behavior therapists themselves to be better able to work with their religious clients. Those clients are in their own ways critiquing the behavioral views being utilized in therapy. By conducting a religious evaluation of the field themselves, the behavior therapist may be made more sensitive to the religious views the client brings to therapy.

The Validity of a
Religious Critique

In this section, I will argue that contemporary approaches to the philosophy of science suggest that a host of nonempirical factors influence (but do not determine) the process of science. The possible influence of religious beliefs and values on science (especially the human sciences) will be discussed. The principal thesis will be that contemporary perspectives on philosophy of science give all persons a certain degree of license explicitly to utilize their religious presuppositions as control beliefs over the scientific process, thus establishing the propriety of the proposed critique of the field of behavior therapy. I will conclude with an examination of significant objections that might be raised against such a critique.

Postpositivistic Philosophies of Science

The essence of the positivistic view of science was ably summarized by Mahoney (1976, p. 130) when he said that the positivistic scientist typically believes that

1. scientific knowledge is grounded in empirical facts which are known for certain;

2. theories are derived from (and therefore secondary to) these facts;

3. science progresses by the gradual accumulation of facts;

4. since facts form the foundation of our knowledge, they are independent of theory and fixed in their meaning;

5. theories (or hypotheses) are logically derived via the rational process of induction; and

6. theories (or hypotheses) are retained or rejected solely on the basis of their ability to survive experimental tests.

Such a positivistic view of science has been slowly eroding for decades. The analyses of science promulgated by historian/philosopher of science Thomas Kuhn (1962/1970) were the first really to catch the imagination of the psychological world, and the psychological literature was replete with pronouncements of "paradigm-busting" studies, paradigm shifts, new paradigms, and so forth for several years. Since that time, many psychologists have become increasingly aware of contemporary "historicist" trends in the philosophy of science, and now hardly an issue of *American Psychologist* comes out without at least one article discussing a new implication of a postconventionalist view of science for contemporary psychology (e.g., Gergen, 1985; Howard, 1985; Manicas & Secord, 1983).

The remnants of positivistic conceptions of the scientific task are probably still more prevalent in behavioral circles than in any other. "Behavior therapy's self-image is that of an applied science, devoid of any prescriptive thrust or any implicit system of values, the essence of which can be accounted for without reference to any cultural or historical context" (Woolfolk & Richardson, 1984, p. 777). Krasner and Houts (1984) provided empirical data to support such a contention, finding behavioral psychologists to be significantly more committed to a factual orientation to their work (as opposed to a theoretical orientation), and more likely to believe in impersonal causation of human behavior, elementarism, physicalism, and quantitative orientation. They were more likely to endorse reductionism, and to reject metaphorical, rational, or generally antiempiricist positions.

A host of competing "historicist" views of science have arisen to replace positivist views. What seems to hold these diverse views of science together is their common attention to the host of *non*empirical factors that shape the scientific enterprise, factors that include cultural and historical factors, values, worldviews, language systems, and the psychology and sociology of science. Quite apart from their real differences in their understanding of the scientific task, these views all contain criticisms of positivistic views of science as failing to take into account adequately these nonempirical factors.

While these different historicist views are diverse and complex, there are two general versions of historicist views: *Realist* views and *Instrumentalist* views of science. Manicas and Secord (1983) and Gergen (1985), respectively, are excellent representatives of realism and instrumentalism among the writings of psychologists. These two classes of views are distinguished by the relative degree of optimism or pessimism they embody regarding the possibility that scientific methods can ever help us truly to know reality. The realist positions acknowledge the influence that the knower and a host of "nonscientific factors" exert upon the knowing process, but nevertheless assert that in some fashion reality can "break through" the knowing process so that human conceptions can (fallibly) reflect the true order of the world. The instrumentalist positions, on the other hand, so emphasize the human nature of the knowing process that they despair of human knowing ever really reflecting reality at all. Gergen thus calls knowledge "an *artifact* of communal interchange" (1985, p. 266) and questions the extent "to which scientific accounts may be (*if ever*) corrected or modified through observation"(p. 273, emphases added in both quotes). For instrumentalists, human knowing (including scientific knowing) is tied up inside the inescapable circle of human psychological processes and never makes real contact with the world.

In the midst of these fertile discussions about the nature of science (though data-minded behaviorists seem frequently to dismiss them as arid), religious belief is only rarely mentioned as a possible influence on the knowing process, and then only by explicitly religious writers such as Wolterstorff (1984). Yet religious beliefs are intertwined with the presuppositions, worldviews, values, political commitments, and so forth that the scientist holds. The fact that so many in psychology make commitments in these and other areas without recourse to traditional religious beliefs or doctrines in no way means that these decisions or beliefs are not in some fundamental way religious. *The punch line is that contemporary understandings of the nature of scientific knowing and methods, by their explicit incorporation of nonempirical influences in their understanding of science, open the possibility that religious beliefs and commitments may have a valid role in the scientific process.*

By delineating four central assertions about the process of scientific knowing that flow from most historicist views of science, I hope to establish a credible base for a religious critique of behavior therapy. Each assertion will be briefly discussed/defended.

Assertion 1: Data Are Theory-Laden

Naive realism, or what Nietzsche called the "doctrine of immaculate perception" (in Mahoney, 1976, p. 133), is simply no longer tenable. No psychologist who knows anything about the human perceptual system can deny that data are presorted or processed from their first "entry" into the human organism. Beyond basic neurological processing, innumerable studies in perception indicate the profound impact that expectancies have upon the perceiving process. The philosopher of science Stephen Toulmin has argued that the scientist "does not (and should not) approach Nature devoid of all prejudices and prior beliefs." Rather, preexisting conceptions "should guide his expectations" as he or she goes about the work of science, with the expectation that evidence will "show him how to trim and shape his ideas further" (Toulmin, 1962, p. 45). The basic assertion here is that, without preorienting conceptions of some sort, we cannot perceive data at all; the world would be a "bloomin' buzzin' confusion." We have data at all only because we sort our experience according to dimensions of relevance to our prescientific commitments. Koch (1981, p. 267) said "We cannot discriminate a so-called variable... without making strong presumptions of philosophical cast about the nature of our human subject matter." Recent attention to gender biases in what male and female social scientists attend to in data collection, in such areas as moral reasoning and socialization, might be cited as a case in point (Gilligan, 1983). Such "theory-ladenness" of the data may be accentuated in the human (behavioral) sciences.

Assertion 2: "All Scientific Theories Are Underdetermined by Facts" (Hesse, 1980, p. 187)

Why do we accept certain theories and reject others? Positivistic conceptions of science suggest or imply that we construct theories inductively based upon data alone or we propose them tentatively and then accept only those that survive critical tests. But there has been significant criticism of such notions in recent times. In the quote above, philosopher of science Mary Hesse was arguing that the "facts" never support one theory and one theory alone; rather, factual and "non-factual" factors such as values held by the scientist go into theory acceptance and adherence.

Further, Meehl (1978) summarized the arguments against the idea of a "crucial test" of a theory. Theories comprise flexible "webs" of assertions that can be shifted easily to resist attempts at theory falsification. For instance, a crucial test of psychoanalysis targeting the occurrence (or nonoccurrence) of symptom substitution can be refuted by casting doubts on the measures of such substitution, the ways in which the need for such substitution was induced, the centrality of that phenomenon to analytic theory, and so forth. One can never test a single aspect of a theory, and thus theories are amazingly resilient against such so-called crucial tests.

The thrust of Assertion 2 is that our acceptance of any particular theory is never a function merely of the data or of the results of experimental challenge. It would seem that the data are rarely scrutinized exhaustively before we commit ourselves to a theory. Rather, in addition to the empirical evidence, a host of nonscientific factors influence theory choices. These influences include what scientists value in a theory ("epistemic values" such as predictive accuracy, internal coherence, and the like; Howard, 1985); the host of nonepistemic values held by the scientist (e.g., feminism, empiricism, rugged individualism, and so forth; see Gergen, 1978); what those we respect and are trying to emulate believe; and the contingencies of the scientific social network (e.g., what can "get published"). In summary, what the (previously theory-laden) data say is only part of what goes into our acceptance of scientific theories, or, as McMullin (cited in Howard, 1985, p. 258) said, "theory-appraisal is a sophisticated form of value-judgment." Making explicit the extrascientific determinants of our theory acceptance and rejection decisions will enhance our own capacities to be honest as a scientific community and to make more accurate judgments. It is my belief that congruence with our religious beliefs is an important factor in our acceptance and rejection of theory.

Assertion 3: Values Shape Our Decisions of Which Areas to Focus Upon for Investigation

This is the most face valid of the four assertions, but it needs to be stated clearly. It is no accident that we investigate ways to prolong ejaculation or enhance orgasm in our culture, and not ways to diminish sexual pleasure; we study assertive self-expression and ignore humility or contemplative silence; we view anxiety as a nuisance to get rid of and not as a means to personal growth through suffering (Evans, 1986). It has been commonly noted that what is studied as a problem to conquer in our culture (e.g., authoritarianism) has been viewed positively in other settings (e.g., Germany in the 1930s). Our values direct where we exert our technical prowess (Sarason, 1984). Frequently, our scientific formulations carry implicit within them a pressing value message by the labels we give them and the way we conduct our research (see Gergen, 1978).

Assertion 4: Worldviews or Control Beliefs Have a Pervasive Effect on the Shape of the Scientific Process

The variety of "extraempirical" factors that shape the scientific process are not a chaotic collage of random beliefs, values, and the like. There is a certain cohesiveness to the fundamental commitments we bring to the tasks of life, leading many to characterize our starting points as "worldviews."

> A worldview (or vision of life) is a framework or set of fundamental beliefs through which we view the world and our calling and future in it. . . . It is the integrative and interpretive framework by which order and disorder are judged, the standard by which reality is managed or pursued. (Olthuis, 1985, p. 155)

In a very general and fundamental way, it tells us both what is and is not the case and what ought to be the case in our world. These foundational commitments or "control beliefs" (Wolterstorff, 1984), are "tacitly assumed in faith rather than deliberately produced through rational inquiry [and these] ultimate answers lie behind all our creative living and thinking" (Olthuis, 1985, p. 158).

Prominent behaviorists are beginning to see that these sorts of basic assumptions are the starting points of all human endeavors, including the endeavor of science. Steven Hayes (1984, p. 205), in a recent book review, asserted that contemporary behaviorists have rejected most forms of logical positivism, and freely noted that behaviorism is itself a "world view (a paradigm, a philosophical approach)," and as such, "it incorporates its own techniques, methods, principles, . . . and philosophical assumptions."

What sorts of elements constitute our worldviews? Olthuis (1985, p. 155) suggests that "biophysical, emotional, rational, socioeconomic, ethical, and 'religious'" elements are present, and each type of factor has different types of influence at different times. There is wide disagreement on which types of such assumptions should exert an influence on the conduct of science. Fletcher (1984) recently discussed the role of fundamental assumptions in the conduct of science, concluding that the only assumptions that had a valid role in science were those that were minimally necessary for the conduct of the scientific enterprise and about which there was unanimous assent in the scientific community. On the other hand, Alvin Plantinga, a recent president of the American Philosophical Association, has argued persuasively that there is no compelling reason for individuals who believe in God not to include the existence of God among the fundamental worldview assumptions brought to the scientific task. Plantinga (1983, p. 14) asserts (and his suggestions for Christian philosophers are meant for all Christian scholars): "The Christian philosopher quite properly *starts from* the existence of God, presupposes it in philosophic work, whether or not he can show it to be probable or plausible with respect to premises accepted by all philosophers, or most philosophers, or most philosophers at the leading centers of philosophy." Ellis and Skinner, among others, have explicitly made disbelief in God a part of the fundamental commitments they bring to the scientific task by virtue of their embracing of a thoroughgoing naturalism. If disbelief can suitably be among the control beliefs of some scientists, it would seem that belief in God and related beliefs could be allowable for others as their control beliefs.

Summary

We come to the task of science as whole human beings who live our lives, necessarily, in the context of a worldview. This worldview is not narrowly religious in the sense of being composed of explicitly dogmatic theological assertions. The worldview is formed out of a host of factors (described by Olthuis above), which include the religious. One aspect of our worldviews is our values, which shape what we care about and, therefore, choose to study as scientists and how we apply our knowledge. Our worldviews shape what we see as data; they shape our expectancies and our basic vision of our existence. We choose theories, and the methods that we use to test them, in the context of our worldviews. We are capable of knowing a real world, and hence are capable of being sensitive to what the data say, but what the data say is only one part of the theory testing and acceptance process. It is my belief that a forthright discussion of the worldview assumptions we bring to the study of the science of human behavior would enrich and deepen our knowing of persons. Contemporary historicist philosophy of science, recognizing the prevalence of the nonempirical factors that shape science, gives us license to evaluate the control beliefs that have shaped a scientific area like behavior therapy. Such an evaluation can only be done in the context of an independent set of worldview assumptions such as those entailed by a Christian religious commitment. That is the task being attempted in this chapter.

Possible Objections to a
Religious Critique

Objection 1: While some science may be "value-laden," good science is not. The basic assertion here would be that science is not *necessarily* shaped by nonscientific factors, but is only so influenced when a science is not mature or when the scientists are not doing a good job in their scientific work. If this is true, then the appropriate response to the discussion about control beliefs and worldview influences would be to redouble our efforts to expunge these nonempirical factors from the scientific realm. There is real merit to this objection, in that those sciences commonly viewed as being more advanced or mature (e.g., physics or chemistry) are perhaps less pervasively influenced by worldview-type assumptions than are the human or behavioral sciences. While discrimination of any data or weighing of any theory is influenced by nonempirical factors, undoubtedly people carry many more presupposed notions into the study of persons than when they approach the study of subatomic particles (most of us having been "lay theorists" about people since birth).

So the various sciences may in fact differ in terms of the pervasiveness and profundity of the influence of worldview assumptions on them, but this might have less to do with the relative "maturity" or "purity" of the science than it does with the inherent complexity and accessibility of the subject matter of interest. Koch (1981, p. 267) argued that "psychology is necessarily the most philosophy-sensitive discipline in the entire gamut of disciplines that claim empirical status." Does this mean that psychology is really less mature or rigorous as a science? Such issues are beyond the scope of this chapter, but it would seem that explicitly incorporating values and worldviews into the scientific process does not necessarily result in a total loss of objectivity or methodological rigor. If it is the case that everyone is operating out of worldview assumptions, and that the influence of such factors is actually inevitable, then the advancement of the scientific enterprise would seem to be furthered better by making those beliefs explicitly available for public inspection and discourse as opposed to denying their existence and influence.

Objection 2: Incorporation of worldviews, including religious presuppositions, into the scientific process is impossible because the two entities (science and religion) are fundamentally incompatible. We frequently hear that (a) science rests on facts, religion on faith; (b) scientific claims are falsifiable while religious claims are not accessible to real life evaluation; and (c) that the criteria for choosing between scientific theories are clear and objective while the criteria for choosing between religions are ambiguous and subjective. If science and religion are that different, how can there be any interaction between them?

Barbour (1974) addressed these purported disjunctions between science and religion, and concluded that none of them hold water. First, he pointed out that science is not based on pure facts but that there is a certain degree of uncertainty involved in all human knowing, and we must assume something to know anything. Religion, on the other hand, is sensitive to certain realities of the human experience, and people sometimes put their religious beliefs to serious test against reality. Brunner (1939, p. 205) said, "The decision about the truth or untruth of the Christian doctrine of man is made in experience." Second, Barbour pointed out that falsifiability is not easy for either science or religion. It is not the case that scientific theories are falsifiable and religious beliefs are not. Finally, he argued that the criteria for theory acceptance and rejection in science are far from clear-cut. Empirical theory testing is part, but not the total sum, of decision making between scientific theories *and* between religions.

Barbour's conclusion was essentially that science and religion are related human endeavors, each of which involves the attempt to make sense out of a very complex existence. He acknowledged a difference in *degree* rather than a true dichotomy between the two activities, with religion necessarily dealing with the more subjective, less easily testable realities of our existence. Such a difference of degree does not, however, constitute an impassible crevasse between the two activities.

Objection 3: Incorporation of religious worldview assumptions in the conduct and evaluation of science could lead to a "religious imperialism" of religion over science. Does the present critique open the door to a "religious psychology" where the dogmatic assertions of systematic theology replace the attempt to test our beliefs against reality, or where science could degenerate into unproductive and endless squabbling about the relative merits of the assumptions of different religions as the starting point for psychological science? Here it must be clarified that religious control beliefs properly operate at very broad and fundamental levels (see Wolterstorff, 1984, chaps. 7, 11, and 14). Religiously influenced worldviews will not "actually contain [the scientist's] theories" (Wolterstorff, 1984, p. 77) and are not the source of the data by which we evaluate our theories even though our worldviews influence what we see as the data (p. 79). These control beliefs are clear enough to lead us to reject some theories and lean toward others (p. 76) but are also broad and vague enough to allow for a diversity of possible theories that may all be compatible with the control beliefs (pp. 78-79). The core task of the Christian scholar is not to derive the substance of a discipline from divine revelation or religious tradition, nor is it to ignore religion in a vain attempt to be totally neutral in doing science. Rather, the task of the Christian scholar is to "study reality in the light of biblical revelation" (Greidanus, 1982, p. 147). A commitment to modesty about the influence of control beliefs and to the possibilities of testing our assertions against reality can prevent such a "religious imperialism."

The Religious Critique

Woolfolk and Richardson's (1984) excellent critique of behavior therapy was conducted from a cultural perspective. Drawing upon "the sociology of knowledge, critical theory, and hermeneutic philosophy" (p. 777), they attempted to survey and critique the cultural and ideological assumptive foundations of behavior therapy. I will be attempting a similar but distinct task, that of evaluating behavior therapy's assumptive foundations from my own religious perspective, that of an "evangelical" Christian.[1] I will not defend that faith position here, but rather merely declare it in order to be consistent with my own call for honesty about the control beliefs that shape the work of the scientist.

It must be emphasized again that the form of analysis I am attempting can be validly conducted from *any* faith perspective. While many of the evaluative comments made below distinctively flow from evangelical Christian presuppositions, the *way* the critique is conducted is a "generic" one. In the following, it is recognized that the field of behavior therapy is quite diverse, embodying applied behavior analysis, mediational conditioning approaches, social learning theory, cognitive-behavioral therapies, and the cognitive therapies.

Determinism and Freedom

It is perhaps easiest to start with a fairly obvious area of disagreement between the behavior therapy and religious communities. Generally speaking, behavior therapists endorse some form of macrodeterminism (Erwin, 1978), the notion that, on the level of human or behavioral events, all behaviors are the inevitable results of the causally relevant conditions that preceded the behavioral event in question. Skinner (1976, p. 185) has said, "A person is not an originating agent; he is a locus, a point at which many genetic and environmental conditions come together in a joint effect." Wolpe (1978, p. 444) suggested similarly that

> delightful as it is to regard ourselves as partially free agents not entirely under the domination of the causal sequences that relentlessly channel the course of events for everything else in nature, this freedom is, alas, only an illusion. Our thinking is behavior and is as unfree as any other behavior. . . . We always do what we must do.

Cognitive-behaviorists frequently take similar stances, as evidenced in a recent statement by Marlatt (1982, p. 333). Speaking about responsibility in the development of an addiction problem, he states that "the fact is that an individual who acquires a maladaptive habit pattern on the basis of past conditioning and the effects of reinforcement is no more 'responsible' for his behavior than one of Pavlov's dogs would be held responsible for salivating at the sound of a ringing bell."

In critiquing this aspect of behavior therapy assumptions, we must ask if Christian belief does necessarily entail a rejection of determinism (i.e., it is not the case that every human event is the inevitable outcome of preceding events) and a correlated belief in freedom (the idea that, on at least some occasions, the person could have acted otherwise given exactly the same prevailing influences on behavior at the time of acting).

There are some Christian groups that embrace such a strong view of God's sovereignty that they could be labeled theological determinists. Such a position is not in keeping with the mainstream of orthodox Christianity. John Calvin is commonly believed to have denied the freedom of persons, but his belief in God's sovereignty cannot be equated with philosophical determinism because he simultaneously asserted a belief in limited human freedom (see his *Institutes*, Book II, chap. 2), an assertion that was intellectually credible in his time because of his embracing of Aristotelian notions of causality as opposed to the Humean notions of causality accepted by most behaviorists (Muller & Vande Kemp, 1985). Perhaps the clearest statement of human freedom in the Calvinistic tradition comes from the Calvinistic *Westminster Confession of Faith* (chap. 11; Leith, 1973), which says "God hath endued the will of man with that natural liberty, that is neither forced nor by any absolute necessity of nature determined to good or evil."

In the Christian tradition, every "human being—to the extent in which he is really a human being—is responsible" (Brunner, 1939, p. 1973). Responsibility for our actions necessarily requires the capacity to have acted otherwise in a given situation, and so, from a Christian perspective, total determinism is unacceptable and limited freedom is an essential belief. Plantinga (1983, p. 23) nicely summarized the essence of a Christian position by defining the concept of "agent causation: the notion of a person as an ultimate source of action." The Christian must believe in some form of agent causation, some notion that the person's choices are sometimes the ultimate and deciding factor in the occurrence of an action, in order to believe that we are truly responsible beings who can be held accountable for our actions before God.

The caricature by behaviorists, that views that assert human freedom destroy any justification for regularity or predictability in human behavior and thus result in a necessarily chaotic view of humanity, is unfounded. In behavioral analyses of the freedom issue, we are frequently told that actions must either be caused by events outside of the behavior itself, or the behaviors must be viewed as uncaused—with the implication that uncaused behavior makes a behavioral science impossible. But it is the false dichotomy of event causation or no causation (i.e., chaos) that is the real problem. In addition to the options of event determination and indeterminism as determinants of behavior, we have the option of agent determination. Also, the choices between causes do not have to be exclusive; to argue that in a particular instance the person is an ultimate cause does not rule out that event causation also affects the behavioral outcome, or that indeterminacy (error variance) isn't among the causes of an action as well. The notion of agent causation also doesn't mean that the choices of a free agent aren't shaped by constitutional or environmental factors. Our freedom is not unbounded: "The being of God alone is unconditioned, absolute freedom; that of the creature is conditioned, relative freedom, freedom in dependence" (Brunner, 1939, p. 262). The Christian concept of freedom is not that of freedom from regularity, freedom from influences upon behavior, or freedom from finiteness. It simply means that, in the final choice that creates the behavior, the chooser was not usually a "locus" of influences coming together, but that he or she decided among real options, influenced as he or she was by his or her history and constitution. This conception of limited freedom is thus explicitly compatible with a nondeterministic form of person-environment interactionism.

Given that freedom is a concern for the Christian, how can we grapple with this tension between the behavioral assumption of determinism and the Christian belief in freedom? Evans (1977/1982) has suggested several typical resolutions. The first is simply to capitulate to the "scientific" assertion of determinism and deny the reality of limited freedom. Another is to embrace theological determinism in order to make macrodeterminism subsumable under a doctrinal belief.

The most common resolution, however, is to redefine freedom to make freedom and determinism *compatible*. This is achieved (e.g., Bufford, 1981, chap. 2) by following Jonathan Edwards and B. F. Skinner in defining freedom as being caused to act in a manner in accord with one's wishes or desires. In this view, a certain action (for example removing money from my wallet and giving it to another) is free if the behavior coincides with my desires (as when I give money to my church) but is not free when it is against my desires (as when I give it to a stranger at gunpoint) *even though my actions in either instance are regarded as causally determined by precisely the same "laws of learning."* What makes the former instance free is not that I could have acted otherwise under the same circumstances (in the behavioral analysis I could not have done so), but that the enacting of that behavior was not unpleasant for me because it was in accord with my causally predetermined desires at the moment. This is obviously an anemic view of freedom, in that both behaviors were inevitable and in neither case could the person have done other than what he or she did. The core problem in such a view is that, in a deterministic understanding of the person, we can never do other than what we do. It would seem that we are stuck with incompatible perspectives on this topic; determinism and limited freedom do in fact appear to be irreconcilable.

Any contemporary discussion of this issue, however, must take up Bandura's (1978) notion of "reciprocal determinism." This concept seems to have almost taken the behavioral world by storm, in that it seems to encapsulate best a human recognition of freedom qualified by a humble recognition of the limitations and constraints on that freedom; a view that seems to mesh well with the Christian view of freedom described above. Bandura (1978, p. 357) himself believes that

> it is within the framework of reciprocal determinism that the concept of freedom assumes meaning. . . . Because people's conceptions, their behavior, and their environments are reciprocal determinants of each other, individuals are neither powerless objects controlled by environmental forces nor entirely free agents who can do whatever they choose. People can be considered partially free insofar as they shape future conditions by influencing their courses of action.

This concept is alluring to the religious person who also believes in limited freedom, but is reciprocal determinism really adequate as an understanding or explanation of limited freedom? Does it embody a substantive understanding of agent causation, or is it in fact a repackaging of the standard conceptions of event causation? Bandura (1978, p. 348) himself stated that "a self system is not a psychic agent that controls behavior." The essence of his position seems to be that the self system is a system of internal or cognitive "mechanisms" (p. 348) that develop through past direct or vicarious experience, judgments by others, and by logic. "[Once] established, self-produced influences operate as contributory factors in the regulation of behavior" (p. 350). Thus the person is not an illusory way station for external causes of behavior, but is rather a substantive processor of the factors that combine together to cause behavior. By emphasizing the triadic intersection of person factors, environment, and behavior, Bandura hopes to restore the person as an important contributor to his or her behavior, rather than being a mere repository of learning history or locus at which causes interact.

But is this real freedom? Note first that Bandura himself does not regard persons as psychic agents, saying that we are not "autonomous regulators of behavior" (p. 352). Note also that even though the proposed self-system is substantive, it is still mechanically conceived, including its development and activation: "External influences play a role not only in the development of cognitions but in their activation as well" (p. 348). "Self-evaluative influences do not operate unless activated" (p. 354). So it appears that, for Bandura, human beings are free in the sense that their behavior has an impact on their environment, and in that their self systems are not mere way stations for environmental influence but rather really mediate environmental influences. Thus the nature of the self system really makes a difference.

But, in Bandura's system, we are not free in the sense of having any choices over which the person exercises ultimate control as a responsible agent; where the person's actions are not totally determined by the environmental events or uncontrollable genetic/biological influences that have controlled the development of the hypothesized self system. Bandura (1983) made this clear in his response to the criticisms of Phillips and Orton (1983) when he said that there is always "sequentiality" of reciprocal influence, meaning that he acknowledged that, ultimately speaking, the behavior that changes our environment is necessarily caused by the preexisting environmental conditions processed by existing person structures. Because the person structures must in turn be caused (in terms of temporal ordering) by environmental factors acting on preexisting biocognitive potentialities, it appears that Bandura's system collapses into an event deterministic framework with more of the causal processes absorbed into the person.

In none of the behavioristic conceptions of the person do we have *true* limited freedom. All of these models are thus "dangerous" in that they propose a view of human persons in which we are mechanisms of some sort or another, beings that always do what they must do. This is as true for Bandura's conception of the person as for Wolpe's. Such views demean our true nature and undermine our sense (which reflects reality) of our responsibility for our actions.

But can a person with a Christian worldview still learn from these models? Yes. Because human freedom is viewed within a Christian framework as a reality rather than a hypothesis, this person would believe that it is necessarily the case that behavioral conceptions of the person, to the extent that they deal with reality at all, are structured to take freedom into account. There is always some "slippage" between metatheoretical conceptions and the specifics of any theory, and this is the case here. Thus, even though at the metatheoretical level behavior therapists embrace determinism, they are nevertheless distinctive among the psychotherapy approaches for being open with clients and trying to enlist the client as a *"collaborator,"* a concept that carries with it a high view of the client's powers of choice. Compared to analytic, Rogerian, and family systems approaches, which seem to have a low view of the person's capacity for meaningful change apart from expert intervention, behavioral approaches have a high view of the person's capacity for change through "self-control" and related processes. So, in spite of the metatheory of determinism, behavioral approaches themselves do not necessarily undermine the freedom of the client unless they are applied deceptively or coercively. The ready acceptance of Bandura's concept of reciprocal determinism seems to me to point to the de facto openness of behavior therapists to recognizing the reality of freedom at a clinical level.

Atomism and Holism

Behavioral conceptions of the person are definitely atomistic, following the British empiricist philosopher David Hume who denied the reality of a substantive "self" or self-identity for the person. The person was instead a bundle of perceptions and impressions held together loosely by human memory. The self is nothing more, in this view, than the aggregation of the person's empirical characteristics.

Such a view is obviously a direct parallel to contemporary behavioral conceptions of the person. Skinner (1971) derided the concept of "autonomous man," preferring to talk about the determinants of specific behaviors occurring under the control of environmental causal influences. In contemporary texts on behavioral assessment (e.g., Hersen & Bellack, 1981), it is not persons that are assessed, it is behaviors and their controlling variables (e.g., S-O-R-C). This may not by itself be problematic as an isolated strategy for understanding a problem, but when elevated to a philosophical postulate, it does create problems from a religious perspective. For example, Bellack and Hersen (1977) said bluntly that "personality is not a real thing" (p. 12), and this is perhaps typical of the behavioral views wherein the person as a unified being disappears to be replaced by a loosely aggregated collection of determined response capacities, whether that aggregate is environmentally determined (Skinner) or is substantively influenced by a self-system (Bandura). In either case, the focus is upon discrete determinants of certain response dispositions, with no attempt to think in terms of the whole person at all.

Does a religious view of the person necessarily dictate the need for a substantive self? Properly understood, it does. The practical outcome of an atomistic view of the person is that there are no necessary interrelationships between discrete components of the person's behavior. The only interrelationships that exist between clusters of behaviors are those that exist by the accident of conditioned association or some such process. There is no necessary grounding of any particular behavior in a self. Thus a concept of responsibility is impossible, because there is no "person" available to hold responsible for the behavior exhibited. Each behavioral pattern has its own specific controlling conditions that bear no necessary relationship to the person as a whole. This is the reason that Lazarus (1977, p. 117) can say so clearly to his client to "think of your 'self' not as one big 'I' but as a whole complex of iiiiiiiiiii's. Each little 'i' corresponds to some aspect of your being." Behavioral clinicians, like Lazarus, frequently counsel clients not to overidentify with any specific aspect of their behavior ("*You* are not a failure, you are a person who failed at one specific task!").

There is a certain clinical wisdom and utility to such an approach, in that the spurious overidentification by a client (as a person) with a particular negative aspect of her or his behavior is genuinely problematic. It is in fact this insight that is of central value for the religious thinker. But Christian thought would nevertheless require the identification of specific behaviors in some nontrivial manner with the unified person, because a person who commits specific behavioral acts that are sins must be capable of validly being labeled a *sinner*. This label must apply not merely in the trivial descriptive sense, but in a more powerful way in which the person's behavioral acts are diagnostic of the inner condition of the "heart" or unified core of the person. In the absence of a unified person, there is no one to hold responsible for sin, and indeed no unified person to be redeemed and sanctified, but rather, only discrete behavior patterns to be modified.

Without such a holistic view of the person, we also encounter major problems from moral and judicial perspectives. How does one punish a response pattern from a judicial perspective? Skinner (1971) is correct in suggesting that, if his view of the person is accurate, we must move away from the concept of justified punishments of persons for their crimes and toward modification of specific behavioral tendencies.

Another major contribution of behavior therapy is its focus upon idiographic assessment of the person. It must be forcibly noted that the acceptance of the necessity of a substantive concept of a unified self does not necessarily make one a trait theorist. The issues of idiographic organization of behavioral tendencies and indeed of the influence of environment on behavior (Mischel, 1973) are logically distinct from the notion of a substantive self. Allport (1955) supported something of a notion of the self, which he called the "proprium," and yet was a strong proponent of the idiographic analysis of the person. The real pragmatic gains of behavioral analysis of personality come from the idiographic approach to personality, which is *logically unrelated* to the positing of a unified self (which may function idiographically or nomothetically), and from the enhanced attention paid to situational determinants of behavior, which is again distinct from the issue of the unified self. Nor does this view of a substantive self necessarily entail the acceptance of a homunculus view of the person wherein one must always attribute behavior to the "unmoved mover" within. A unified notion of the person may be subjected to analysis and explanation, but not to a form of analysis that by its very methods denies the reality of the person it studies.

Fundamental Motivations

Though rarely discussed expressly, one cannot survey the behavioral literature without perceiving that human beings, and in fact all living organisms, are viewed as being motivated principally to enhance their own welfare; that is, egoism is assumed to be the primary motivation of all human behavior. This is perhaps best seen clearly by examining some classic problem areas for egoism—love and altruism—to see how behaviorists deal with these areas.

Behavior therapists rarely talk about love, but they have been very active in developing clinical models of the functioning of marriages. Central to all discussion of marriage from a behavioral perspective is the concept of *reciprocity*, the notion that individuals tend, over time, to match exchange rates of reinforcers and punishers to maximize reinforcement for themselves (see Jacobson & Margolin, 1979, chap. 1). Stuart (1980, p. 370) codified this as one of his central notions in understanding marriage, one that he called "the best bargain principle: The behaviors that all parties in relationships display at any given moment represent the best means that each person believes he or she has available for obtaining desired satisfactions." So at the bottom level, even in that most "giving" of human relationships—marriage—persons are characterized as only out to maximize their own receipt of personal satisfactions.

The same is true in the area of altruism. Kanfer (1979) offered one among several available behavioral conceptualizations of altruism, in which altruism was analyzed principally as a form of self-control behavior wherein one can learn to delay receipt of personal and immediate reinforcement for the sake of outcomes that are more distal, thus "maximizing the potential for individual satisfaction *and* group survival" (p. 235). "[The] task, as in self-control, is to train persons to act for the benefits of another because it is in their own self-interest" (p. 237). The core assumption here is that humans are ultimately incapable of acting in a manner contrary to their own self-concerns.

It should be briefly noted that the assumption of egoism or selfishness does not just affect discussions of love or altruism but has a broad impact on all considerations of human action. For example, most considerations of interpersonal behavior from a behavioral perspective use the organizing conception of "competency" to understand the function of interpersonal action. This concept leads us to understand human behavior as necessarily and primarily directed at obtaining some desired good from the environment. Competent responses are most often defined as those that are "effective" at getting what we want or at accomplishing a specific "task" (see McFall, 1982). Behavioral theories and concepts direct our attention inexorably to the *functional* value of any human behavior; what it "does for" the organism.

There is a difference between trivial and nontrivial egoism, one that is critical to this analysis and that is cogently explained by Wallach and Wallach (1983). The trivial version of egoistic thought says that ultimately we do anything because we "want to do it," whether it is giving to the poor to the point of our own poverty or pursuing the materialistic American dream. But egoism becomes nontrivial when it is suggested that not only do we act because we want to, but also that "all that can ultimately affect our satisfaction or pleasure is the fate of our own internal needs" (Wallach and Wallach, 1983, p. 202). In the above analyses, it seems obvious that the behavior therapists cited are suggesting not just that people give to their spouses or to others in general because they want to do so (trivial egoism), because this leaves open the possibility that one can genuinely act for another's welfare without regard for his or her own. Rather, they are making a much stronger claim that what matters ultimately to human beings is only their own need gratification (nontrivial egoism). If I find it reinforcing to love my spouse and give to her, I only find it to be so because of the returns such behavior produces for me. I cannot really care for another individual in a self-sacrificing way; if what I do seems self-sacrificing, it is only because the reinforcers controlling my behavior are not obvious.

How does such a view mesh with a Christian view of the person? In some ways, Christian theology is quite pessimistic about unredeemed humanity, and the notion of a basically selfish understanding of the human race is broadly compatible with such a view. But there exists a balancing conception in theology that must be contended with, that being the notion that we are all created in the Image of the God of all love, the giving, self-sacrificing God. Any Christian thinker should be reluctant to dismiss the human capacity for true compassion and self-sacrificing love. The love described in I Corinthians 13 is definitely not a self-interested love devoid of personal sacrifice. Love is a foundational human capacity created in us from the beginning, as when the first humans in the creation story were told to cleave to one another, and that the two would become one flesh. Descriptively, the Christian scriptures and tradition seem to take human selfishness into account, appealing, for example, to the rewards we will personally receive in heaven to motivate good behavior here on earth. But the scriptures never stop at that point, and call a person on to a life wherein his or her desires come to conform evermore to God's purposes without regard for his or her own welfare.

In summary, the Christian view of the person, of marriage, and of interpersonal relationships in general seems descriptively to take human self-interest as a basic fact of human existence, but does not assume (as does behavioral theory) that human beings are incapable of ever truly caring for something beyond themselves regardless of its impact on their personal welfare. Such a view of motivation fails to account adequately for what human beings are and might become. To the extent that psychological theories not only describe behavior but also *prescribe* how people *ought* to view themselves, the behavioral view of our fundamental motivations might actually be destructive to humanity by lowering their expectations to the point where they can never escape the closed circle of selfish self-preoccupation.

Rationality

The value of rationality. The manner in which rationality is valued in behavior therapy was ably discussed by Woolfolk and Richardson

(1984). Founded as it was upon a logical positivist base denying the meaningfulness of any proposition that was not verifiable, it comes as no surprise that embedded in behavior therapy is an exalted prizing of rationality and a proportional devaluing of the nonrational, emotive, and intuitive aspects of human life. They note that emotion is generally viewed as something to be managed, averted, extinguished, and generally controlled by the behavior therapist. Most cognitive-behavioral models of therapy (unlike their operant counterparts) assume the rationality of the client and the amenability of his or her problems to rational resolution.

Does a Christian view of the person put reason in a similar place in human experience? On the one hand, Christians such as Aquinas, Calvin, and most Catholic and Reformed theologians have historically viewed rationality to be a major aspect of what it means to be created in God's image, and thus have placed a high value on that rationality. Most Christian traditions have also noted that this capacity for rationality was marred in some form by the fall into sin of the human race. The result of this fall for Aquinas was that perfect rationality was contaminated by a necessary linking of reason with a fallen will; for Calvin, reason itself was contaminated with sin. In either case, rationality remains a valued human capacity that must be striven for. But rationality is not seen as the premier human capacity in most Christian traditions. In a sense, rationality remains ever subject to the human heart.

It is quite difficult in this area to understand properly the intended meaning of the biblical writers who did not write in the precise language required in contemporary science and theology but in the practical and phenomenological terminology of their day. Contemporary biblical and theological scholars seem to concur, nevertheless, that, in the biblical revelation, the Hebrew and Greek concepts of mind (or reason) and heart are somewhat overlapping, with heart clearly being the super-ordinate concept (Brunner, 1939, pp. 224-225; McDonald, 1982, p. 24). The concept of "heart" in most biblical references (e.g., "And you shall love the LORD your God with all your heart" Deuteronomy 6: 5) refers to the central, vital, unified center of human nature. The heart is the person as a whole, of which rationality is a part. And it is clear that the heart, this unified center of the person, is never conceived of as purely rational in biblical usage—"The heart is more deceitful than all else and is desperately sick; who can understand it?" asks the prophet Jeremiah (17:9). Neutral, objective rationality, while treasured in Christian tradition, is not the center of what it means to be a person. Humans are thinking, willing, acting, valuing, feeling, believing beings, and the nonrational aspects of our natures must not be subjugated to pure rationality. So Christian presuppositions would necessarily lead the person studying behavior therapy to balance out the rationalism of behavior therapy with a respect for our nonrational attributes.

The standards of rationality. Behavior therapists' definitions of rationality follow the historical definitions of science present at the founding of behavior therapy by endorsing pragmatic standards for rationality. I will here use Ellis's Rational Emotive Therapy (RET) as a case example to support this point. While Ellis's system may not contain as careful definitions of rationality as, for instance, Aaron Beck's, Ellis's system is relatively easy to critique and is here used as an example of how the standard for rationality used in any system may be critiqued.

Ellis's definitions of rationality have evolved over time, but a consideration of the different formulations is instructive. Prior to about 1978, Ellis utilized two different standards depending upon his purposes at any given moment. The first standard for the rational was a pragmatic one: "By *irrationality* I mean any thought, emotion, or behavior that leads to self-defeating or self-destructive consequences that significantly interfere with the survival and happiness of the organism" (Ellis, 1977a, p. 15). Second, Ellis (1977b, pp. 220-221) endorsed "empirical" or "scientific" standards for rationality:

> The rational-emotive therapist . . . teaches the general principles of scientific method and logic to his clients. . . . He is in many such ways a scientific interpreter who teaches his clients . . . how to follow the hypothetico-deductive method and to specifically apply it to their own value systems and emotional problems.

Thus those beliefs that are warranted after testing by the scientific method are rational, and those that do not pass the test are irrational.

The problem is that these two different standards are each internally incoherent and are not compelling in and of themselves. First, we can note that the pragmatic standard as stated is not very helpful. Happiness is not defined, and happiness and survival (the two values mentioned within the pragmatic standard) can conflict, as when a person comes to feel that they must embark upon a particular course of action to preserve their self-respect (happiness), and that course of action puts their survival at risk (as when a person believes she must testify against a member of a hostile street gang active in her own neighborhood). The scientific standard by itself is not very helpful either, because, as noted previously, the core assumptions of logical positivism are self-stultifying; the idea that a belief must be verifiable by scientific method to be meaningful is not in itself verifiable and hence is not meaningful. It may be that few assertions that are meaningful can be completely verified, and it may be difficult to specify clear criteria for when some assertion has sufficient backing to warrant believing it. Neither the pragmatic nor scientific standards are internally coherent and are not compelling. To make matters worse, Ellis tends to use one standard without regard for the other depending upon which fits his purposes at the moment.

Further, the independent pragmatic and scientific standards can also conflict. Suppose a person in Nazi Germany was told to believe that the Jews were the children of Satan. Such a belief is clearly not scientifically respectable, but it would certainly optimize survival in that setting to believe it! We may have to risk our happiness and survival to believe something because of the scientific evidence for it. On the other hand, it may be essential for human happiness to believe in something (e.g., the existence of God) that is not amenable to empirical proof.

Ellis (1978, 1982), however, has altered his standards slightly. Stating that "RET posits no absolutistic or invariant criteria of rationality," he more recently asserts that the term *rational* refers to "people's (1) setting up or choosing for themselves certain basic values, purposes, goals, or ideals and then (2) using efficient, flexible, scientific, logico-empirical ways of attempting to achieve such values and goals" (1978, p. 40). While it may well be an improvement in RET if Ellis has in fact become less absolutistic about what true rationality is, it really doesn't seem that he has changed. On the following pages of the 1978 article, he proceeds to question any human contact with the transcendent (p. 41), denies life after death (p. 42), endorses "humanistic-existentialistic" philosophy (p. 47), and, most important, says that "if people want to stay alive and enjoy themselves . . . they *need to seek several important goals. R.E.T. therapists try to help their clients achieve these goals*" (p. 55). He then proceeds to list the same values that have always guided RET practice. This is hardly a retreat to an accepting stance regarding others' value positions.

The point in all the foregoing is to suggest that it is impossible to judge rationality without a standard by which rationality is measured, and most standards for rationality in behavior therapy really are little different from Ellis's. His standards are unacceptable from the perspective of a Christian view of persons because they are poor standards in and of themselves, and because they lead to conclusions about the nature of human existence that are at variance with the Christian worldview.

Is there a single, focal, and exclusively Christian view of what it means for an assertion to be rational? No. Christian views of rationality will, however, prominently feature the compatibility of human belief with divine revelation as *one* principal criterion for true rationality. It should not be presumed that Christian belief entails a naive notion that religious faith ever assures perfect rationality. The divine revelation (the Bible), though inspired by God, is limited in scope ("Its purpose is not encyclopedic but redemptive," Holmes, 1977/1983, p. 53) and is interpreted by fallible human beings. Nevertheless, Christians do believe that we can know truth because we were all created by the God of all Truth to be able to know God. Holmes's (1977/1983) book *All Truth is God's Truth* is a helpful discussion of knowing truth from a Christian worldview.

In summary, behavioral views of rationality are a step in the right direction, in that, unlike dynamic and other approaches to psychotherapy that underestimate the capacity for rationality of the human species, behavior therapists take rationality and its place in living a productive life seriously. A Christian view of the person would put reason in the context of other human capacities and would necessarily posit standards for rationality other than those proposed by Ellis (none of them "cut-and-dried").

Classic Humanism and Christian Humanism

Woolfolk and Richardson (1984) identify behavior therapy as embodying the ideals of "classic" humanism, which they identify as an "allegiance to the primacy of science and reason in intellectual affairs, [opposition to] all irrational authority and arbitrary privilege, and ... a dedication to the promotion of human freedom and happiness" (p. 781). A related but unmentioned postulate of behavioral humanism is its reliance upon humanity to change itself; as Skinner (1971, p. 206) said, "We have not yet seen what man can make of man."

Christian humanism differs from classic humanism. It also embodies a high view of the person, but sees the value and the equality of all persons as rooted in our being created in the image of God. Quoting extensively from Brunner (1939, p. 344):

Thus there is a "Christian humanism," by which we . . . mean . . . the knowledge of and insistence on the unity of humanity, and of the particular dignity and divine distinctiveness of man's being which is based upon the center of the Biblical revelation. Genuine Christian humanism is based upon the fact of the Incarnation of the Son of God. . . . [Man] is singled out by the Creator in an unparalleled way as the one in whom the Creation has reached its summit, whose redemption, therefore, is also the aim and the meaning of the whole of history. Man—not the Aryan, not the male, not the civilized man, not the bearer of spiritual values, not the superman of the future—but all who bear the human face.

From the perspective of Christian humanism, science and reason, rather than being autonomous and self-sufficient, are viewed as being dependent upon God for their veracity as discussed earlier. As to the sufficiency of humanity to change itself for the better apart from God, the Christian humanist is more a pessimist than an optimist. The individual with a Christian view of the person must see people as capable of meaningful change and as capable of doing good, but such changes would be viewed as occurring within definable limits. If the capacity for change represents the core of what it means to be free, then Christian humanism truly embraces a paradox: "The maximum of his dependence on God is at the same time the maximum of his freedom, and his freedom decreases with his degree of distance from the place of his origin, from God" (Brunner, 1939, p. 263).

The person embracing a Christian worldview cannot, therefore, embrace the classic humanism described by Woolfolk and Richardson, but he or she can exhibit a high appreciation of human equality and value, a genuine excitement about the contributions of science and reason, and some optimism that humans can change for the better, with that optimism enhanced where God is involved in the change process.

**Amorality and the
Ideals That Guide Action**

Amorality . . . refers to the modern separation of fact and value. . . . The goals of traditional psychotherapy were provided in large measure by theories of personality that supplied some definition of what people ought to be and a picture of optimal human functioning. . . . [Behavior therapy] is neutral with respect to what would constitute a personal ideal or ideal person. (Woolfolk & Richardson, 1984, pp. 780-781)

Behavior therapists basically embrace a different "metamorality," one of freedom and tolerance (Woolfolk & Richardson, 1984, p. 781), with the result that the behavior therapist essentially (and ostensibly) allows the client totally to determine the course of therapy. Behavior therapists, consequently, seem better at eliminating suffering (about which clients have focused goals) and much less proficient at conducting "growth-oriented" therapies because clients are frequently unclear about how to grow and the therapist has officially eschewed all models of optimal human functioning. The behavioral notion of optimal functioning one would gain from a survey of behavioral journals would include *painlessness and competency to solve problems and obtain reinforcement*. It would posit no common characteristics of the "healthy" person, but would focus only on the outcomes obtained by that individual's behavior.

Christianity, on the other hand, is prescriptive at its core. It proposes what the optimal life would look like and sketches the broad framework for how we can arrive at that place. Many biblical passages could epitomize this prescriptive element of Christianity (the interested reader might examine, for example, Phillipians 3:7-11). The prescriptive nature of the Christian life focuses both upon outcomes obtained by the person (e.g., a relationship with God, salvation, the resurrection from the dead) and on character achieved by virtue of one's commitment to the Creator-Redeemer (e.g., lovingkindness, humility, and self-control).

In a modern age in which the specification of any clear prescriptive beliefs violates the metamorality of freedom and tolerance, such a clear prescriptive focus of religious faith may sound anachronistic, dogmatic, and intolerant. But as Woolfolk and Richardson (1984, p. 783-784) noted,

> With the advent of modernity, those institutions that once provided a sense of meaningful conduct, and the inability of modern consciousness to fashion some intersubjective consensus on metaphysical questions have led to considerable psychosocial stress . . . and philosophical disorientation. . . . Behavior therapy, as it is presently constituted, is unable to further the search for meaning.

If one's moral commitments run in the direction of tolerance and freedom, behavior therapy is proportionately more appealing. From a Christian perspective, the lack of prescriptive focus actually can allow for more comfortable utilization of the system by the religious believer as compared to a system more encrusted with its own explicit and well-developed vision of optimal humanity.

Conclusion

My goal in this chapter has been to conduct a critical analysis of some of the assumptions behind a major contemporary approach to the understanding and change of the human person from the perspective of a religious worldview. My belief in doing such an analysis is that the whole field of psychology would benefit from a clearer elaboration of the worldview-type foundations for the way we see the human condition, for our proclivities in terms of theory acceptance and rejection, and for the values that direct our choices of problems to be researched and modified. These are not purely empirical matters, but are rather intimately intertwined with how we answer those ultimately religious questions concerning the nature of human existence, the puzzle of the causes of human suffering, the relationship of humans to that which transcends us, and our notions of how we can remedy the tragedies of the human condition.

In spite of the critical tone of the foregoing, I want to close this chapter by again asserting that I am a Christian behavior therapist. As I approached choosing a way to help people change, I first had to confront the inadequacy of Christian presuppositions alone to guide the practice of psychotherapy. While the presuppositional basis for a Christian approach to the person is laid out in the scriptures, the presuppositions and assertions about persons in the Christian worldview are insufficiently precise to guide scientific theory construction or therapeutic practice (Berkouwer, 1962, p. 194; Brunner, 1939, pp. 61-62; McDonald, 1986). So I had to look for a model that would be sufficiently compatible with my metatheoretical presuppositions to allow for productive use of the approach.

In behavior therapy, I found an approach that posited limited freedom for the person (even if the precise understanding of that freedom was incompatible with a Christian understanding of freedom). I found an approach that coincided well with my notions that the embodied, human aspect of our existence was important and which had a well articulated understanding of the person variables and processes which were foundational to human action. Though the atomism of behaviorism was unacceptable, the idiographic style of behavioral conceptualizations of the person seemed respectful of human uniqueness and to be compatible with the empirical data in that area. I also felt that a certain degree of functional autonomy of response patterns within the self was compelling, especially when compared against dynamic approachs which seemed to understand human behavior in extremely rigid nomological fashions, with all behavior relating intimately to central unconscious causal states. An appreciation of the influence of the environment upon behavior seemed compelling. A certain level of egoism did seem present in all human behavior, and that certainly seemed like the place one must often start the change process for pragmatic reasons. Behavior therapy had a high view of rationality which I valued, and it didn't seem hard to modify the standards of rationality for my purposes. The humanism of the approach seemed in line with my instinct first that many of the people I would be working with would not be interested in incorporating God into their change process, and secondly that I could not force God into a procedure in therapy anyway so that God's involvement in therapy would have to occur by standards God would set, not I. The amorality of behavior therapy was actually an advantage in that it allowed me to establish my own values and ideals for human growth without being forced to premature closure by my work with a theory. Finally, as a Christian, I was committed to good stewardship of my time and energies, and so it seemed natural to embrace an approach to therapy which emphasized empirical accountability in all aspects of its practice.

Worldview assumptions are primary. Rational discourse about our assumptions is possible and important. Rational proof of them according to some sort of foundationalist standard (Wolterstorff, 1984) is not possible. For all of us, our worldview assumptions came before our adoption of behavioral theories, and our worldviews are reciprocally affected by the theories we adopt as they shape what we see as the data. A clear articulation of the interaction between worldviews and what we see as data, the theories we endorse, and our values will enrich both our scientific and therapeutic work. Such an interplay between the worlds of psychology and religion, while having a long and distinguished history (Vande Kemp, 1984), has much yet to add in the future to enriching the work of all behavioral scientists.

NOTE

1. For those unfamiliar with evangelical Christianity, the following set of conceptions comprise what I believe to be the core of the "evangelical" Christian position which are

relevant to the present analysis: God, the personal, loving, just, and sovereign LORD of the Judeo-Christian scriptures, exists. God is separated from the creation, yet is intimately involved with our lives, and sustains our very existence. God created all that is, including the human race (the means by which that creation was accomplished is for our purposes irrelevant). Human beings are created in the Image of God. We are embodied beings whose lives transcend the merely physical. We were made male and female. We are capable and are in fact inevitably interrelated with the Creator God. We are rational beings, capable of knowing truth, and God has revealed truth to us and also made us capable of discovering truth. God made us and values us, and hence we have value. We are endowed with limited freedom, making us responsible moral agents. As responsible agents, we all have rebelled against and thus need God's forgiveness, and can only find true life in relationship with God through Christ, God's son. We are given purposes in this life, which can be summarized as bringing glory to God through our work and our lives. In all of life, we are to reflect God's character in our persons (see McDonald, 1982).

REFERENCES

Allport, G. (1955). *Becoming*. New Haven, CT: Yale University Press.

Bandura, A. (1978). The self system in reciprocal determinism. *American Psychologist, 33*, 344-358.

Bandura, A. (1983). Temporal dynamics and decomposition of reciprocal determinism: A reply to Phillips and Orton. *Psychological Review, 90*, 166-170.

Barbour, I. (1974). *Myths, models, and paradigms*. New York: Harper & Row.

Bellack, A., & Hersen, M. (1977). *Behavior modification: An introductory textbook*. New York: Oxford University Press.

Berkouwer, G. (1962). *Man: The image of God* (D. Jellema, Trans.). Grand Rapids, MI: Eerdmans.

Brunner, E. (1939). *Man in revolt* (O. Wyon, Trans.). Philadelphia: Westminster.

Bufford, R. (1981). *The human reflex: Behavioral psychology in biblical perspective*. San Francisco: Harper & Row.

Calvin, J. (1981). *Institutes of the Christian religion* (H. Beveridge, Ed. and Trans.). Grand Rapids, MI: Eerdmans. (Original work published 1559)

Ellis, A. (1977a). The basic clinical theory of rational-emotive therapy. In A. Ellis & R. Grieger (Eds.), *Handbook of rational-emotive therapy* (pp. 3-34). New York: Springer.

Ellis, A. (1977b). A rational approach to interpretation. In A. Ellis & R. Grieger (Eds.), *Handbook of rational-emotive therapy* (pp. 216-224). New York: Springer.

Ellis, A. (1978). The theory of rational-emotive therapy. In A. Ellis & J. Whitely (Eds.), *Theoretical and empirical foundations of rational-emotive therapy* (pp. 33-60). Monterey, CA: Brooks/Cole.

Ellis, A. (1982). A reappraisal of rational-emotive therapy's theoretical foundations and therapeutic methods: A reply to Eschenroeder. *Cognitive Therapy and Research, 6*, 393-398.

Erwin, E. (1978). *Behavior therapy: Scientific, philosophical, and moral foundations*. Cambridge: Cambridge University Press.

Evans, C. (1982). *Preserving the person: A look at the human sciences*. Grand Rapids, MI: Baker. (Original work published 1977)

Evans, C. (1986, January 17). The blessings of mental anguish. *Christianity Today*, pp. 26-30.

Fletcher, G. (1984). Psychology and common sense. *American Psychologist, 39*, 203-213.

Gergen, K. (1978). Toward generative theory. *Journal of Personality and Social Psychology, 36*, 1344-1360.

Gergen, K. (1985). The social constructionist movement in modern psychology. *American Psychologist, 40*, 266-275.

Gilligan, C. (1983). Do the social sciences have an adequate theory of moral development? In N. Haan, R. Bellah, P. Rabinow, & W. Sullivan (Eds.), *Social science as moral inquiry* (pp. 33-51). New York: Columbia University Press.

Greidanus, S. (1982). The use of the Bible in Christian scholarship. *Christian Scholar's Review, 11*, 138-147.

Hayes, S. (1984). But whose behaviorism is it? [Review of *Behaviorism, science, and human nature*]. *Contemporary Psychology, 29*, 203-206.

Hersen, M., & Bellack, A. (1981). *Behavioral assessment: A practical handbook* (2nd ed.). Elmsford, NY: Pergamon.

Hesse, M. (1980). *Revolutions and reconstructions in the philosophy of science.* Bloomington: Indiana State University Press.

Holmes, A. (1983). *All truth is God's truth.* Downer's Grove, IL: InterVarsity Press. (Original work published 1977)

Howard, G. (1985). The role of values in the science of psychology. *American Psychologist, 40*, 255-265.

Jacobson, N., & Margolin, G. (1979). *Marital therapy.* New York: Brunner/Mazel.

Kanfer, F. (1979). Personal control, social control, and altruism: Can society survive the age of individualism? *American Psychologist, 34*, 231-239.

Koch, S. (1981). The nature and limits of psychological knowledge. *American Psychologist, 36*, 257-269.

Krasner, L., & Houts, A. (1984). A study of the "value" systems of behavioral scientists. *American Psychologist, 39*, 840-850.

Kuhn, T. (1970). *The structure of scientific revolutions* (2nd ed.). Chicago: University of Chicago. (Original work published in 1962)

Lazarus, A. (1977). Toward an egoless state of being. In A. Ellis & R. Grieger (Eds.), *Handbook of rational-emotive therapy* (pp. 113-118). New York: Springer.

Leith, J. (Ed.). (1973). *Creeds of the churches.* Richmond, VA: Knox.

Mahoney, M. (1976). *Scientist as subject.* Cambridge, MA: Ballinger.

Manicas, P., & Secord, P. (1983). Implications for psychology of the new philosophy of science. *American Psychologist, 38*, 399-412.

Marlatt, G. (1982). Relapse prevention: A self-control program for the treatment of addictive behaviors. In R. Stuart (Ed.), *Adherence, compliance and generalization in behavioral medicine* (pp. 329-378). New York: Brunner/Mazel.

McDonald, H. (1982). *The Christian view of man.* Westchester, IL: Crossway.

McDonald, H. (1986). Biblical teaching on personality. In S. Jones (Ed.), *Psychology and Christian faith: An introductory reader* (pp. 118-140). Grand Rapids, MI: Baker.

McFall, R. (1982). A review and reformulation of the concept of social skills. *Behavioral Assessment, 4*, 1-33.

Meehl, P. (1978). Theoretical risks and tabular asterisks: Sir Carl, Sir Ronald, and the slow progress of soft psychology. *Journal of Consulting and Clinical Psychology, 46*, 792-805.

Mischel, W. (1973). Toward a cognitive social learning reconceptualization of personality. *Psychological Review, 80*, 252-285.

Muller, R., & Vande Kemp, H. (1985). On psychologists' uses of "Calvinism." *American Psychologist, 40*, 466-468.

Olthuis, J. (1985). On worldviews. *Christian Scholars Review, 14*, 153-164.

Phillips, D., & Orton, R. (1983). The new causal principle of cognitive learning theory: Perspectives on Bandura's "reciprocal determinism." *Psychological Review, 90*, 158-165.

Plantinga, A. (1983). *Advice to Christian philosophers.* (Available from the author, Department of Philosophy, University of Notre Dame, South Bend, IN)

Sarason, S. (1984). If it can be studied or developed, should it be? *American Psychologist, 39*, 477-485.

Skinner, B. (1971). *Beyond freedom and dignity.* New York: Bantam.

Skinner, B. (1976). *About behaviorism.* New York: Vintage Books.

Stuart, R. (1980). *Helping couples change.* New York: Guilford.

Toulmin, S. (1962). *Foresight and understanding.* San Francisco: Harper.

Vande Kemp, H. (1984). *Psychology and theology in Western thought (1672-1965): A historical and annotated bibliography.* Mill Wood, NY: Kraus.

Wallach, M., & Wallach, L. (1983). *Psychology's sanction for selfishness: The error of egoism in theory and therapy.* San Francisco: Freeman.

Wolpe, J. (1978). Cognition and causation in human behavior. *American Psychologist, 33*, 437-446.

Wolterstorff, N. (1984). *Reason within the bounds of religion* (2nd ed.). Grand Rapids, MI: Eerdmans.

Woolfolk, R., & Richardson, F. (1984). Behavior therapy and the ideology of modernity. *American Psychologist, 39*, 777-786.

9

Behavioral Psychology and Religion

A Cosmological Analysis

E. MANSELL PATTISON

The overall theme of this book is to demonstrate viable relationships between behavioral psychology, its theory and practice, and religious faith, belief, and practice. Whereas other chapters have examined particular and specific relationships, in this chapter, I plan to present a more global overview. Precisely, I wish to view these relationships in a historical and cosmological perspective.

In a recent literature review of religion and mental health, I found singularly few references to behavioral psychology (Pattison, 1978). How might we account for this lacuna in a literature with perhaps over 10,000 citations? It is surely not that behavioral psychologists are unaware of religion, nor that religionists are unaware of behaviorism. Without any documentation to support my personal impressions, it seems to me that both groups have *not* ignored each other, but rather have been content to make snide asides—without direct confrontation.

Behaviorist Cosmology

The behaviorist remarks might be of the genre that all behavior is the consequence of specific conditioning. Therefore, religion possesses no transcendent value or truth, given that personal religion is the conditioned response to socialization within religious institutions. To the

American father of behaviorism, circa 1910-1920, J. B. Watson is attributed the apocryphal boast: "Give me a child until the age of six, and I shall determine his behavior for life." Such claims lay within the *Zeitgeist* of late nineteenth-century and early twentieth-century thought-forms. To wit, the concept of a divine providence in a divine universe had long since given way to the rationalism (even skepticism) of Enlightenment thought. Humanity no longer existed in a universe with the divine, linked in covenantal relationships. Rather, from the philosopher Hume onward, humankind existed in a mundane universe. Human relationships were not mutual covenants, reflective of the holy covenant between the people and God. Instead, rational humanity contracted with one another to construct their own universe. Science was the handmaiden of this cosmology. The tools of science, grounded in the philosophies of empiricism, rationalism, logical positivism, and operationalism, would provide the means whereby humankind could rationally and empirically construct the best possible universe. The particular twists of this philosophical cosmology produced the optimistic concept of social evolution: that culture was gradually improving and becoming more sophisticated and urbane. Humankind was evolving into higher and better forms of personhood and social relations (Brandsma et al., 1986).

In late Victorian England, these thought-forms promoted the notion of rational social planning. In turn, the young science of psychology looked hopefully to contribute to a rational plan for human development. This was prominently featured in the blooming of human eugenics. Psychologists averred they would develop tests to identify inferior humans (to be eliminated) and identify superior humans (to be proliferated). It would be hard to differentiate the authorship of such "eugenic breeding" tracts in turn-of-the-century England from the later racial superiority tracts of Nazism.

Corollary to the breeding of superior humans was the need to then train such humans in a rational way to perform rightly in the service of creating superior societies. Evil acts (or at least socially destructive acts) were to be interpreted as the product of either poor breeding or poor training. If we could not immediately eliminate poor breeding, at least we could eliminate poor training. Hence the immediate social appeal of Watsonian behaviorism.

A further piece of cosmological thought was advanced by the American prophet of behaviorism, B. F. Skinner. It is noteworthy that Skinner was born and reared in a conventional Methodist family of the early twentieth century. Although precise details are not available, at least a surmise may be made about this influence on the work and thought of Skinner. At that point, American Methodism was the center point of the development of the "social gospel." Such Methodist theology, in American context, eschewed traditional transcendental theology. Rather, it was devoted to "reforming society," to "improving society," to "redressing social ills and evils." In a word, the Methodism of the childhood of B. F. Skinner partook of the same cosmology of philosophy and science of the times (Ahlstrom, 1972).

This brief sketch on the cosmology of behaviorism suggests that religion has not been ignored, but rather that religion was reinterpreted as just another variable of social conditioning (Skinner, 1953).

Religious Reactions to Behaviorism

It is not uncommon to hear casual aspersions upon behaviorism by religious leaders. Usually such remarks share the general public abhorrence toward a programmed society. But what is striking is the general lack of understanding of behavioral principles, and the lack of detailed scholarly religious scrutiny of behaviorism. We may consider two seemingly antithetical explanations for this situation, both rooted in American values and traditions.

On the one hand, American culture is rooted in the notion of individualism and self-determinism. The American myth that "anyone can become President," or anything else one sets a mind to, states a fantasied self-omnipotence that flies in the face of the fact that we are *not* born with equal opportunity or equal potential. The idea of predetermined limits, or constraints imposed on us by early social conditioning, is not syntonic with this American myth. In its overly simplistic forms of conventional understanding then, behaviorism is casually dismissed as a naive view of human nature that lacks credibility. Or said scientifically, simpleminded behaviorism lacks "face validity." For example, I questioned a random group of college students about behaviorism. Their responses were of this sense: "Oh yes, it explains a few things—but it's pretty simple." To these college students, the image of a behavioral psychologist was someone with a stopwatch or a wrist-counter making minute observations on trivial aspects of behavior.

On the other hand, I suggest that religionists have not examined behavioral psychology closely (as they have existential psychology and psychoanalysis), because the cosmology of behaviorism may be quite comparable to the latent cosmology of American religious thought. I have in mind the fact that the American ethos was founded on the notion of a theocracy. Although religious freedom was a rallying cry, in fact, Puritan New England was an experiment in social engineering to create the perfect society here on earth. Puritan child-rearing practices were manifest exercises in conditioning of mind and behavior, to fulfill the mandate of the book of Proverbs to "train up a child in the way he should walk, and when he is old, he will not depart therefrom" (Warren, 1966).

The history of American religious movements has been a succession of religious utopian visions, and experiments in the creation of "religiously programmed societies." This religious cosmological agenda can be discerned apart from theological or religious *content*. In earlier history, we have the liberal utopia of Ralph Waldo Emerson and the conservative utopias of the Mennonites, Amish, and Shakers. In contemporary times, we have visions of national utopias in religious garb: the liberal version of social gospel redemption in the Democratic party off-shoot of the "Rainbow Coalition," and the conservative version in the Republican party offshoot of the "Moral Majority." Both versions promote the vision of a homogeneous program for achieving a socially engineered ideal society (Viner, 1972).

Is it too farfetched to suggest that religionists of all stripes may avoid an examination of the philosophical cosmology of behaviorism, lest it expose the fact that it is their own agenda?

Science and Faith: Research and Practice

Another facet of our analysis is the relationship between scientific theory and religious faith, belief, and practice. More technically, we wish to consider the relationship of their epistemologies.

First, consider the nature of scientific knowledge. Today we stand as the inheritors of a century of conventional wisdom about science. Perhaps we have less unquestioning faith in the validity and reliability of scientific data—although just recently I met with a group of seminary students who seemed to have incredible beliefs that science was the source of infallible truths. Science still has a mystique about it. And science as a methodology is still confused with "scientism"—a philosophical epistemology of truth.

Indeed, nineteenth-century science was imbued with "scientism": the belief that science was the ultimate source of ultimate truth. As Jean-Paul Sartre caustically remarked: the nineteenth-century French philosophers saw science as replacing theology, and, therefore, the idea of God could safely be discarded as a costly and useless hypothesis. Sartre was not so sanguine, for said he, if there be no God, then humanity is left to its own devices with no one to turn to for truth, and, therefore, humankind is alone, forlorn, abject, and absurd (Sartre, 1947).

The twentieth century has seen the waning of "scientism." Led by Ludwig Wittgenstein in the 1920s, philosophy turned from the "big, ultimate questions" that were perceived as "unanswerable by the scientific method." Instead, the agenda of philosophy was to be the "process of asking questions." The task became asking logical questions, not producing "truthful answers." *Pari passu*, such "process philosophy" has invidiously become the philosophy of science. Science can no longer be perceived as seeking and providing "TRUTH" in any ultimate sense. Science provides proximate, tentative, process "truths."

In fact, science has come full circle. Science cannot be relied upon to explain much beyond the immediate experimental context, much less life and the universe. The anthropologist Claude Lévi-Strauss (1966) has wryly observed that, if one wants an explanatory system for all the events of life, one is much better off to accept the explanatory cosmology of a primitive tribe, for the "primitive mind" has an explanation for everything, while science has an explanation for hardly anything!

With this backdrop, I turn to examine the sciences of human behavior vis-à-vis religion. In Table 9.1, I have compared each of the major behavioral science disciplines in terms of its theoretical views of religion, the amount of research considered on religion, and the religious adherence of members of each discipline (Pattison, 1978).

We note that anthropology and sociology both apprehend religion as a major component of human affairs. Thus a scientific understanding of human behavior is assumed to include how religion plays a significant function in the overall structure of life.

Psychology, as a discipline, does not ascribe such centrality to religion, which is apprehended as a "compartment," not necessarily related to overall human structure and function.

TABLE 9.1
Behavioral Science and Religion

Discipline	Theoretical Importance of Religion	Yearly Scientific Studies of Religion	Percentage of Discipline Personally Religious
Anthropology	Central Theory	1000-1500	1
Sociology,	Major Theory	1000	1
Psychology	Secondary Theory	500	5
Clinical Psychology & Psychiatry	Minor	50	30-40

When we come to the clinical disciplines, the theoretical importance of religion is almost nonexistent in *clinical theory*. In fact, religion is treated as an epiphenomenon unrelated to the basic processes of human behavior. In turn, there is virtually no research on religion in the primary clinical literature.

Juxtaposed to theory and research, we find an inverse relationship with personal religious adherence. Behavioral scientists, qua scientists, perceive the importance of religions as a scientific variable, and proceed apace assiduously to conduct scientific research on religion, despite the fact that they rarely have personal religious commitments. This is a "proximate" view of religion. That is, such scientists are not concerned with the ultimate "truths" of religion, but rather focus on the structure and function of religion in human behavior.

This "process" approach to the scientific study of religion is frequently misunderstood by religionists. It is perceived as "explaining away" religion, or failing to appreciate the truth claims of religion. And indeed such may be a consequence—although not necessarily so. Scientific objectivity is partly myth, and partly a two-edged sword. Partly a myth, in the sense that scientific methods, observations, facts, and deductions are always, in part, a reflection of the scientist and his or her perspectives on the world. Hence, it would be hard to sustain the notion of the "purely" objective scientist. Thus the scientist who holds *any* particular view on religion (pro, con, neutral) may bias his or her approaches to research. Yet the ideals of scientific objectivity are eminently desirable. For empirical data, given their limitations, can serve as a much needed corrective to religious biases. Our scientific research may sustain religious assertions we thought questionable; or research may cause us to question religious assertions (Berger, 1979).

Hence we still have to confront the claims of science and the claims of religion. In my view, neither can lay epistemological claim to superiority over the other. Yet each can complement the other as means to an understanding of the world and our relationships. In theological terms, science explores the "general revelation" of nature, and theology explores the "special revelation" of the biblical corpus (Ramm, 1960).

To return to Table 9.1, we note that the clinical practitioners have a substantial membership who are personally religious. On an intuitive level, such practitioners frequently recognize the importance of religion in the lives of their patients and clientele. Yet we also note that clinical theory has almost no conceptual framework for the comprehension of religion, and almost no pertinent research on religion is generated in the clinical literature (Larson et al., 1984).

This state of affairs presents a number of problems. In brief, clinical practitioners tend to separate into ideological camps. Those clinical professionals who have no personal truck with religion view religious faith and practice as irrelevant to the clinical context; those clinical professionals who are substantively religious seek to imbue their clinical practice with a religious context.

In neither instance may fair appreciation of the place of religion in human affairs be achieved. Religion is viewed through ideological glasses. From a clinical standpoint, both the ardent opponents and the supporters of religion are viewing religion in "ultimate truth" terms. In turn, the actual function of religion in the lives of actual patients may easily get lost.

It is exactly here that a "behavioral" appreciation of religion may play a critical role. By "behavioral," I mean here the observation and analysis of exactly how religious beliefs and practices demonstrably play a role in a person's life. This might include attitudes of faith, transcendent values of life, moral commitments, rituals of religious practice, and the everyday comportment of behavior. Thus I cast a broad net over what we shall consider the "behavioral analysis" of religion (Wuthnow, 1979).

Now some religionists become quite uneasy about the idea that one's religion should be placed under the scientific or clinical microscope. Such activity is viewed as "questioning the unquestionable." Although such concern is understandable, I find it untenable. Certainly from a scientific and clinical point of view, we must honestly scrutinize all behavior of life—including religious behavior, if we are to comprehend the human condition. And from a theological point of view, the failure to scrutinize our own religion is to run the risk of lapsing into idiosyncratic and autistic religion at best; or more subtly retreating into "religious gnoticism"—asserting that the religious components of life are "unknowable."

Finally, the fact that we have no viable clinical theory that embodies religious dimensions is a critical problem for the clinical disciplines. The lack of an articulated synthesis of behavioral psychology and religion is manifestly apparent—but there is just as great a deficiency in all aspects of clinical theory.

Behavioral Psychology and the Psychology of Persons

In this section, I shall briefly indicate the place of behavioral psychology in our understanding of persons. There are three major conceptual approaches to describing persons: the behavioral, the psychodynamic, and the experiential. Each offers a distinctive and valid perspective on the human being. Yet each in itself is inadequate. We must combine all three perspectives to comprehend the humanity of persons.

The behavioral perspective describes the human being in terms of public action, that is, human actions that can be determined by observation without the subject's self-report. Such behaviors are universal in that the same operation (e.g., speech rate) can be observed in all humans. Therefore, these behaviors are *public universal* phenomena.

The psychodynamic perspective describes the human in terms of theoretical intrapsychic human actions. Such actions are inferred from the subject's self-report. This description is private in that it depends upon the subject's willingness to provide a self-report of the experience from which psychodynamic actions are inferred. Such psychodynamic constructs are also universal, however, in that they can be reported by every person (e.g., the report of guilt feelings indicative of superego action). Therefore, the psychodynamic construct actions are *private universal* phenomena.

The personal experiential perspective describes the human in terms of those operations that are private, available only through self-report. As phenomena, they are unique experiences. I describe *my* own experience operating as a human being. Thus personal experience is idiosyncratic. We may recognize a *similar* experience of another, but I can never have your personal experience. Therefore, personal experiences are *private unique* phenomena.

Each of the above three perspectives is necessary, but none is sufficient in itself to describe the person. The behavioral perspective ignores the richness of psychodynamic process and describes the human only in terms of impersonal universal mechanisms. The psychodynamic perspective focuses on internal private processes that may or may not predict behavior outcome, while again these are impersonal universal mechanisms. The personal experience perspective gives credence to unique personal phenomena, but ignores the universal mechanism described in behavioral and psychodynamic analyses (Pattison & Kahan, 1986).

A person is a person. No one conceptual framework affords us sufficient and necessary data to comprehend that biopsychosocial unity that is a person (Carrithers et al., 1985). Science, by its very operations, tends to separate and fragment. And, therefore, each of the three perspectives will separately yield rich, but fragmented pictures of the human person. We have yet to arrive at a synthetic view of personhood that gives due credence to each disparate data base, but yields a holistic or whole view of the person. (Most attempts at holistic views are more mystical and ephemeral than synthetic and integrative, hence holistic psychology is more apparent than real.)

The practical implication of this discussion is to point out that no understanding of religion and spirituality can be approached solely in terms of any one of the three major conceptual approaches defined here. Each perspective affords *some* appreciation of religion. Only by combining behavioral, psychodynamic, and experiential perspectives can we approach an overall appreciation of religion and the person.

In sum, the behavioral perspective is no more and no less important than the psychodynamic and experiential in our approach to religion. Behavioral psychology is a necessary, but not a sufficient, component of our descriptions of humanity and the affairs of religious faith, belief, and practice.

On the Definition of Religion

We turn now to the fact that "being religious" is not a simple concept to define. Simple unidimensional definitions of religiosity fail—because the concept of "religiousness" is just that—a concept. How do we define,

TABLE 9.2
Dimensions of Religion

Dimension	Characteristics	Major Denominational Emphasis
Ideological	Commitment to social cause or movement	Unitarian "civil religion"
Intellectual	Adherence to sets of beliefs or cognitive construction	Calvanists Baptists
Experiential	Feeling experiences Charismatic events	Pentecostals
Sacramental	Participation in sacramental ritual expressions of faith	Roman Catholic
Consequential	Adherence to religiously defined standards of conduct	Fundamentalism

scale, and measure this concept of religiousness? The most popular and accepted analysis is a five-factor typology, developed by Glock and Stark (1965). As shown in Table 9.2, we may consider "being religious" as some combination of "factor-loading" of each of five variables. Put simply, not everyone is religious in the same way.

Much acrimonious disagreement among religious adherents is *not* fundamentally about theology, but rather a difference in the weight of importance given to each of the five factors of "religiousness." As also shown in Table 9.2, different American religious denominations might be sorted according to the strongest weights each gives to a different dimension of "being religious."

Consequently, when we seek to ask: how does religion affect the life of a person, we can give no simple answer. For each "style of being religious" will have a different function in the lives of persons. Rather, we must pose more complex questions like: how is being religious in a certain way likely to influence a person in what ways?

Religion and Behavior

Given that the focus of this book is upon behavioral psychology, it is appropriate to take one aspect of religion—behavior—as an observational point, to comment on the influences of religion.

The potency of religion in the influence of human behavior is related to the level of cultural organization and complexity. On the one extreme, we have the small face-to-face village that is the existent society and the culture, even if there be similar villages nearby. Here, there is a low differentiation of social roles and a relatively homogeneous social existence. In such a society, religion is the culture and culture is the religion. Religion is infused into every aspect of daily life and provides an overarching structure for existence. Here, "religion-culture" defines meaning and action to everything. All of life is ipso facto religious. In such "small societies," there is relative uniformity and conformity. There is early and rigorous socialization into the religious beliefs and practices, for they are the warp and woof of existence. One could scarcely function without being religious. Although deviant behavior can and does occur, the limits of deviancy are severely constrained by the survival needs of the society. In turn, substantial deviancy from the religious-cultural norms is high risk for survival. Where else can one go and survive?

Somewhere intermediate is the small-town phenomenon as part of a large and differentiated culture. The small town retains the essential social homogeneity of the village. Religion and culture are one, despite the superficial variations between local denominations. The social history of small towns in America reflects the paramount importance of immediate personal interaction and insulation from the pluralistic values and life-styles of urban industrialized society. Lingeman (1980) notes that the insular small-town society first came under attack at the turn of the twentieth century when economic subsistence and viability in these small societies were compromised by larger socioeconomic developments on a national scale. Seeking survival in the urban society, the expatriates might feel displaced and long to return to the security and safety of the structured religious culture of the small town. Others, like Sinclair Lewis in *Main Street* and Edgar Lee Masters in *Spoon River Anthology*, satirized the coercive social structure of small-town religious culture. The perceived oppression of small-town mores, however, is from the perspective of the cosmopolitan and pluralistic culture of urban society.

In this case, deviancy from the small-town cultural construction of reality becomes possible and feasible for two reasons. First, there is an available alternative reality of urban society against which to measure the small-town reality. Second, there is an alternative culture to which the small-town deviant can flee—and even be nondeviant in the alternative society.

The same process has obtained in urban areas in both Europe and America, in which small-town religious culture has been re-created in "urban villages," more often termed shtetls, barrios, or ghettos. Urban villagers function with the same tensions of cultural collision as their country village cousins. Some members find comfort, solidity, support, and meaning in the urban village, while others find it stifling and coercive.

The point is obvious here that the village structure is maintained, whether in country or city, by a uniform religious culture that maintains a viable structure of meaning and demands relatively homogeneous behavior of community members. High behavioral compliance is required to maintain village viability in the face of the larger impinging cosmopolitan culture. Personal value is lodged in shared beliefs and values, shared styles of behavior, and shared ideology. Your social role is determined before your birth and remains throughout your life. Who you are in the established continuity of social order is more important than what you do. Therefore, the social task is to learn your ascribed role and live in it. Such is the nature of compliance to a predestined social religious role.

In contrast, the urban cosmopolitan culture is not based on continuity or on similarity. This is a highly differentiated society of multiple tasks and roles. Social role is achieved and lost with equal rapidity. Beliefs, values, and ideologies take a distant second place to the immediate utilitarian performance of tasks that anonymously link with the tasks of others. As a result, the structure and function of the utilitarian culture is not threatened by divergent and pluralistic beliefs, values, and ideologies. Even deviant behavior does not threaten the culture or the individual—"just so long as you get your job done." Thus a religious culture is not necessary for the production of goods and instrumental services. Religious compliance is intrinsically less relevant to the instrumental achievement tasks. Religion and culture can be separated. And for this reason, religion is indeed increasingly irrelevant to urban man, and religion is less potent. On the other hand, the very anonymity of the impersonal urban society role performance makes religion all the more relevant to personal meaning and personal social relations. This process leads to highly "personalized religion"—typical American concepts of personal relations between man and God. Yet this option, too, fails to address the need for "social religion," which links fellow man to fellow man. Again, this is reflected in the characteristic nature of religious resurgence, which stresses religious community. In this latter case, we arrive at religious norms that define the totality of all events and behavior.

The functions of religious compliance in directing behavior and modifying deviance can be seen as a system of human guidance. The linking of religious systems to psychological function in each of the previously mentioned levels of cultural organization is described in detail in *Religious Systems and Psychotherapy* (Cox, 1973). In summary, religious compliance is both strong and central to the agrarian peasant culture. Religious compliance is attenuated in the urban or country small-town society. While religious compliance is impotent and irrelevant to urban utilitarian achievement culture, the relevance of religious compliance to personal meaning and interpersonal relations becomes paramount.

To the extent that a religious organization addresses the multiple spheres of life activity, the more such a religious structure will affect the lives of people. The one extreme case would be the religious commune that withdraws from the urban society and establishes a separate religious culture. Here, there is the demand for total religious compliance in a total religious community. At the other extreme is the case of civil religion, which addresses no specific aspect of actual life behavior. Here, there are no norms to comply with or any social religious structure that can construe religious behavior.

Behavior and Spirituality

It is beyond the limits of this discussion to elaborate fully on the notion of "spirituality." I take this concept to describe the person who seeks to live life in accord with his or her religious principles (Pattison, 1984a).

To my mind, such a full-orbed spiritual commitment would embody fully each and every one of the five dimensions of "religiousness" outlined in Table 9.2. Thus we do not conceive of "spirituality" as some ephemeral quality of being linked to an equally ephemeral "spirit."

It is worth noting that much of conventional Western religious thought about the nature of persons is derived from Platonic philosophy—and not from the Judeo-Christian corpus. In his famous essay ("Phaedrus"), Plato described the human in the following metaphor:

The human is like a chariot (the body), pulled by unruly horses (the emotions), with the driver the pure essence (mind). In this fragmenting analogy, Plato managed to disembowel the biopsychosocial unity of the human person—and we have tried to put the person back together for 2000 years.

If we are to consider spirituality as a condition of personhood, then spirituality is robustly a biological, psychological, and social-behavioral concept. We are spiritual in person (Pattison, 1984b).

It is appealing to hope that religion or religious movements would be integrative and synthetic, in contrast to the fragmenting dispositions of both philosophy and psychology. But the history of religious movements, which after all are products of the human enterprise, reveals the same fragmenting disposition (as illustrated in our discussion of the five dimensions of religiosity). My own personal interpretation of this state of affairs is that religious movements only reflect the inherent fragmenting disposition of fallen human nature. Luther put it nicely when he said: "For we do err daily and sin constantly." Therefore, I always expect that religious movements will in spirit and ideal search for and strive toward coherence—and always fail. I read the history of religious movements as a constant drift in human action away from the ideal, with a series of historical attempts at reform, revitalization, and renewal. Thus there is a religious ebb and flow as we humans scurry like ants to "put it all together."

Here then, I should like to make a radical distinction between *religion* and *spirituality*. By "religion," I shall point toward all that we can scientifically observe of human action. By "spirituality," I point toward the transcendence of human morality. I refer specifically to the notion of the supernatural, and explicitly exclude the popular theological game of talking about ideas about transcendence. Thus *spirituality* shall be defined in my terms as an affirmation of living within a personal commitment of "faithing" in the supernatural. (This is radically different from cognitive religious beliefs, ideas, or concepts.) The great church historian, Jaroslav Pelikan, has observed that the radical transformation of the Reformation was the replacement of "faith" as the basis of religion by "belief." At that point, the existential person of faith became the cognating brain of beliefs.

A number of recent sociologists of religion as well as philosophers of religion have noted that religion is, and should be, the object of study by the scientific method; whereas faith and spirituality are not so—such cannot be adduced or reduced by the scientific method. This is a critical distinction, not universally accepted by all scientists, however. Nevertheless, I shall hold to that company of scholars who reject the reductionism of equating religion with spirituality.

This leads to my concluding commitment to affirm the central role of spirituality in our analysis. From the standpoint of religion, I observe myriad permutations of humankind "pulling themselves up by their own bootstraps." It is only in a transcendent spirituality that affirms the salvation of the human spirit by that which is beyond and apart from us (shall we dare name it God?) that the fragmented human is offered the salvation of our being.

REFERENCES

Ahlstrom, S. E. (1972). *A religious history of the American people*. New Haven, CT: Yale University Press.

Barbu, Z. (1960). *Problems of historical psychology*. New York: Grove.

Berger, P. (1979). *The heretical imperative: Contemporary possibilities of religious affirmation*. Garden City, NY: Anchor.

Brandsma, J. M., Pattison, E. M., & Muyskens, J. L. (1986). Roles, contracts, and covenants: An analysis of religious components in psychotherapy. In D. K. Kentsmith, S. A. Salladay, & P. A. Miya (Eds.), *Ethics in mental health practice*. Orlando, FL: Grune & Stratton.

Carrithers, M., Collins, S., & Lukes, S. (Eds.). (1985). *The category of the person: Anthropology, philosophy, history*. London: Cambridge University Press.

Cox, R. H. (1973). *Religious systems and psychotherapy*. Springfield, IL: Charles C Thomas.

Glock, C. Y., & Stark, R. (1965). *Religion and society in tension*. Chicago: Rand McNally.

Larson, D. B., Pattison, E. M. et al. (1984). Systematic analysis of research on religious variables in four major psychiatric journals: 1978-1982. *American Journal of Psychiatry, 143*, 329-334.

Lévi-Strauss, C. (1966). *The savage mind*. New York: Basic Books.

Lingeman, R. (1980). *Small town America*. New York: G. P. Putnam.

Pattison, E. M. (1978). Psychiatry and religion circa 1978: Analysis of a decade. *Pastoral Psychology, 27*, 8-25, 119-141.

Pattison, E. M. (1984a). Toward a psycho-social-cultural analysis of religion and mental health. In R. C. Nann et al. (Eds.), *Mental health, cultural values, and social development*. Boston: Reidel.

Pattison, E. M. (1984b). The concept of evil in psychoanalysis. In M. Coleman & M. Eigin (Eds.), *Evil, self, and culture*. New York: Human Sciences Press.

Pattison, E. M., & Kahan, J. (1986). Personal experience as a conceptual tool for modes of consciousness. In B. B. Wolman & M. Ullman (Eds.), *Handbook of states of consciousness*. New York: Van Nostrand, Reinhold.

Ramm, B. (1960). *General and special relevation*. Grand Rapids, MI: Baker Book House.

Sartre, J.-P. (1947). *Existentialism and human emotions*. New York: Philosophical Library.

Skinner, B. F. (1953). *Science and human behavior*. New York: Free Press.

Viner, J. (1972). *The role of providence in the social order*. Princeton, NJ: Princeton University Press.

Warren, A. (1966). *The New England conscience*. Ann Arbor: University of Michigan Press.

Wuthnow, R. (Ed.). (1979). *The religious dimension: New directions in quantitative research*. New York: Academic Press.

About the Contributors

JAMES R. BAUGH, Ph.D., is in the private practice of clinical psychology in Jackson, Mississippi. He is Director of Turning Point Outpatient Addictions Program and of Woman's Hospital Eating Disorders Unit. He has teaching appointments at the University of Mississippi Medical Center and Millsaps School of Management. He has written three books: *Solution Training, How to Lose the Farm and Cope with It in Ten Easy Lessons,* and *No Other Gods Before Me: The Healing of Addictions.* He is an Episcopalian and is involved in the church at the parish and diocesian levels.

ALLEN E. BERGIN is Professor of Psychology at Brigham Young University, and former Director of the Values and Behavior Institute there. He is a Fellow of the American Psychological Association, past-President of the Society for Psychotherapy Research and of the Association of Mormon Counselors and Psychotherapists, and a member of the Society for the Scientific Study of Religion. He is a diplomate in clinical psychology of the American Board of Professional Psychology and serves on the Professional Board of the American Mental Health Foundation. Among his more than 60 articles and books are two classic volumes, *Handbook of Psychotherapy and Behavior Change* (with Sol Garfield) and *Changing Frontiers in the Science of Psychotherapy* (with Hans Strupp).

CHARLES R. CARLSON, Ph.D., is an Assistant Professor of Psychology at Wheaton College, Wheaton, Illinois. He received his graduate training in clinical psychology at Vanderbilt University and completed his clinical residency in behavioral medicine at the University of Mississippi Medical Center, Jackson, Mississippi. He has published professional articles in the areas of physiological self-regulation and the role of emotions in social behavior. Currently, he is engaged in the development of techniques enabling effective treatment of stress-related disorders. He and his family are active in the Presbyterian church.

PAUL W. CLEMENT, Ph.D., is Professor of Psychology, Associate Dean for Professional Affairs, and Director of the Psychological Center at the Graduate School of Psychology, Fuller Theological Seminary. For more than 20 years he has conducted research on the outcome of child therapy with special emphasis placed on peer- and self-administered interventions for shy, hyperactive, and aggressive children. He has published 85 articles, chapters, films, and books. He has served as president of the Christian Association for Psychological Studies— Western Region, is on the editorial board of the *Journal of Psychology and Christianity*, and is an ordained Presbyterian elder. He received his Ph.D. from the University of Utah in 1965.

STANTON L. JONES, Ph.D., is Associate Professor and Chairman in the Department of Psychology at Wheaton College, Wheaton, Illinois. He has authored a number of articles in behavior therapy in various journals and recently edited *Psychology and the Christian Faith: An Introductory Reader* (Baker Book House, 1986). He received his Ph.D. in clinical psychology from Arizona State University in 1981. He is a member of the Episcopal church.

JOHN E. MARTIN, Ph.D., is Professor of Psychology at San Diego State University and Associate Professor of Psychiatry at the University of California at San Diego School of Medicine. He is the former codirector of the Joint Doctoral Program in Clinical Psychology at SDSU and UCSD, and recently completed a term as Associate Editor of the *Journal of Applied Behavior Analysis*. His writings include over 60 professional articles, book chapters, and one book in the area of behavioral medicine and health psychology, particularly on behavioral approaches to prevention and control of cardiovascular disease through exercise, smoking treatment, diet modification, and stress management. Since 1984 he has been active in the Methodist and Presbyterian churches in Jackson, Mississippi, and San Diego, California.

WILLIAM R. MILLER, Ph.D., is Professor of Psychology and Psychiatry and Director of Clinical Training at the University of New Mexico in Albuquerque. His writings include a dozen books focusing on the treatment of addictions (*The Addictive Behaviors, Treating Addictive Behaviors*), psychology and religion (*Practical Psychology for Pastors*), and self-help (*Living as If: How Positive Faith Can Change Your Life, How to Control Your Drinking*). He is an ordained Presbyterian elder, and received his Ph.D. in clinical psychology from the University of Oregon in 1976.

E. MANSELL PATTISON, M.D., has been Chair of the Department of Psychiatry at the Medical College of Georgia in Augusta. Previously, he was with the Department of Psychiatry and Human Behavior at the University of California, Irvine. He has authored numerous books and articles on the interface of psychiatry, psychology, and religion.

ELLIE T. STURGIS, Ph.D., is an Assistant Professor of Psychiatry and Behavioral Sciences at the Medical University of South Carolina and Program Director of the Alcohol Dependence Treatment Program at the Charleston VA Medical Center. Her professional writings include over 30 articles and book chapters focusing on behavioral medicine, anxiety disorders, and addictions. She received her Ph.D. from the University of Georgia in 1979. She is active in the Methodist Church.

NOTES

NOTES

NOTES